STORE
WINDOWS THAT SELL

VOLUME 7

STORE

WINDOWS THAT SELL

VOLUME 7

Edited by Martin M. Pegler, SVM

RETAIL REPORTING CORPORATION • NEW YORK

Retail Reporting Corporation
302 Fifth Avenue
New York, NY 10001

Distributors to the trade in the United States and Canada
Van Nostrand Reinhold
115 Fifth Avenue
New York, NY 10003

Distributed outside the United States and Canada
Hearst Books International
1350 Avenue of the Americas
New York, NY 10019

Library of Congress Cataloging in Publication Data:
Main entry under the title: Store Windows That Sell/7

Printed and Bound in Hong Kong
ISBN 0-934590-57-5

Designed by Bernard Schleifer

Contents

Introduction

To promote is to publicize. To present is to show anything at its very best. Promotional Presentations are Displays that are keyed into special events, new looks, new colors, new trends, holidays, seasons — whatever. Promotional Presentations are what make images, what convey concepts and what, in the end, makes sales. That is what Display is all about — and that is what this edition of Store Windows That Sell is all about.

This book is a reference book. It won't get dated and it won't become passe — not so long as "black" comes back every year, so long as there are holidays like "Easter" and "Father's Day," and kids have to get ready to go "back to school." We have planned the book alphabetically — not by the retail calendar — but by words and expressions that always seem to be current in promotions and in the displays of those promotions. We have attempted to cover most of the major selling seasons, the sales events, the sales promotions like "Bridal," "Formalwear" and "Imports" — and the gift-giving times like "Mother's Day" and "Valentine's Day." The book starts with "Accessories" and "Animal Prints" and ends with the "W's": "Western Wear" and "White." Wherever possible we have made references to other areas in the book where the reader may find more ideas that can be adapted to that particular promotion, such as to look under "Denim" for more ideas on "Western Wear."

This is not a book solely developed to women's wear. Included in this seventh edition is an extensive section on menswear displays that range from casual to sports to business to formal wear — as well as the fashion accessories for "him." Even under headings such as "Cruise," "Leather," and "Navy," the reader will see examples of menswear as well as women's wear. Also in this volume there is a section on "Home Fashions & Furnishings," "Jewelry" and "Cosmetics." With mall displays becoming a m ore and more important area for mass merchandise displaying, there are several pages showing some excellent examples of displays created on center court stages and platforms in up-scaled malls.

To explain and show off these ideas for promotional displays, we have selected material from all over; from all parts of the U.S. — from large and small department and specialty stores — from mom 'n' pop shops — from London, Paris, and Munich — from the assorted Americas. As in our previous books we have tried to utilize displays that are weighted heavily with humor, imagination and novelty but still easy and light on the limited budget.

Do you have a promotion coming up? Just check through the index for a word or term that might tie in with your promotion; "Prints and Patterns"? "Black and White"? "Cruise/Resort"? "Navy"? Find the page and see all the graphic "idea-starters" — the displays that will help you to come up with your own unique display. OR — just turn the pages of the book and become acquainted with the wonderful world of display. You can never tell just what you may find that may take you off on your very own special display fancy.

We truly believe that this edition of Store Windows That Sell, with its hundreds of pictures and ideas, will be a book you will savor and then treasure forever as your Thesaurus of Display Ideas.

Martin M. Pegler, S.V.M.

STORE

WINDOWS THAT SELL

VOLUME 7

A

ashion Accessories are the little things that mean a lot. They complete an outfit — they add color where there is no color — they provide the panache and pizazz that can turn a simple, no-nothing dress or suit into a stylish, up-to-the-minute costume. The right accessories can update a dress — revitalize a suit and sparkle last year's outfit with the shimmer and shine right out of this month's *Vogue* or *Harper's Bazaar*. The fashion accessories — the shoes (see Shoes) — bags, gloves, belts, hats and the costume or real jewelry (see Jewelry), are the exclamation points of the fashion statement.

In these displays, the accessories — here scarves and bags — are presented on their own — without the costume they will eventually highlight. Whether the scarves are wrapped around a decorative dress form — or folded and framed as pieces of artwork — or hung out on elegant clotheslines — they manage to suggest the richness of pattern, the drapability and texture of fabric — and the all-important spectrum of colors they come in.

C

B

A: **Escada, E. 57th St., New York, NY**
   Gregory Khoury, Display Director

B: **Galeries Lafayette, E. 57th St., New York, NY**

C: **Gucci, Fifth Ave., New York, NY**
   James Knight, Corp. Dir. of Visual Presentation

D: **Liberty of London, London, England**
   Paul Muller, Director of Promotions and Visual Presentation
   Russell Crook, Designer
   Paul Raeside, Photographer

D

The dress form (A) provides the body for the extravagant wrap of scarves and for the selection of quilted bags with gilt chains that hang off the neck of the form which is already burdened with many strands of faux pearls. At the foot of the form; shoes and some handbag alternatives.

(B) The Galerie Lafayette display makes use of an Empire chair which provides an elevation for the presentation of some of the accessories while the black satin covered dress form beside it wears poufs of colorful scarves, a belt, and a massive piece of costume jewelry. In this beautifully arranged tableau, the viewer's eye travels from the form, at eye level, to the chair and then following the draped scarf on the bag — onto the floor and the casually laid down pink gloves.

The setting in the Liberty of London window (D) is architectural and strikingly neutral in black and white which only makes the brilliant colors of the scarves, bags and umbrellas seem even more so. The soft drape of the scarves — the relaxed and easy look of the tilted bags and the tied-on umbrellas all break out and belie the formality of the setting.

A: Gucci, Fifth Ave., New York, NY
James Knight, Corp. Dir. of Visual Presentation

B: Cole Haan, Fifth Ave., New York, NY
Judy Hamlin, Dir. of Visual Display
Design: Julin & Larrabee, New York, NY

C: Gucci, Fifth Ave., New York, NY
James Knight, Corp. Dir. of Visual Presentation

D: Fendi, Fifth Ave., New York, NY

A

B

C

The accent is on handbags—and in some cases on the shoes that are often shown with them.

Accessories are usually small and are often best presented in shadow boxes — or smaller windows like (A) and (C) where the viewer's eye is immediately focused onto the product being displayed. When the window is taller and larger the designer can, as in (B) add props or decorative elements at above eye level which the viewer can immediately see and then, with a good composition and design, bring the sight level down to the merchandise arranged on assorted height elevations. The use of the multi-level presentation makes each cluster or arrangement of shoe and "go-with" bag become an entity; part of, yet apart from, the other coordinated groups being shown. In the Gucci display (A) the miniature dress forms are sashed with scarves and they, the forms, act as separators between the similar bags.

The Fendi window (D) is a towering window and to show off the bags and accessories, the display designers have created an exciting tableau using nude classic male "sculptures" in a stone finish, and they carry — rather than wear — the assorted handbags, luggage and the leather coats. The window is bathed in a rich, golden light that even further enhances the color of the leather products.

It is music in the night at Lord & Taylor (B): A symphony of shimmer and shine and a single jeweled bag is elevated in song on to the equally be-spangled G-clef — all in the total blackness of the shadow box setting. The lighting does play up the brilliance of the sparkling surface of the bag and the elevating symbol and it sends out rays of light beyond the confines of the limited space.

A fan, hidden from view, sends a soft breeze wafting through the Gucci window (C) and the soft chiffon moves with the oscillating air. Three decorative wire-frame chairs seem to have been "blown over" by the breeze thus gaining greater attention from the passers-by on Sloane St. for the three bags displayed on the scarf bedecked seats of the tilted chairs. A coordinated shoe to "go-with" the pouchy bag it sits on top and adds another accessory note to the "gone with the wind" illusory display. The neutral wall and the black and white checkerboard floor add "class" to the merchandise.

A

Accessories that sparkle when the sun sets and the lights go on all around town. Here are two approaches to the presentation festive evening accessories.

In a deep red ambience, the Saks Fifth Ave. window (A) makes use of neutral colored dress forms with gilded finials to show off the extravagant black and white evening wraps and stoles. The wrought iron, black chair is upholstered in black and white and it carries some small evening bags elevated off the floor. A spray of black feathers crowns the chair back. On the floor — near the cast iron bases of the forms — is a striped black and white pillow used to carry another accessory — and also catch the overflow of the sheer black scarf dripping off the form. The unique wall lamp adds to the evening setting.

B

C

D

From Fendi (D) another high-rising display to match the space of the show window. Large flower pots are painted red, yellow and white and they are arranged pyramid fashion in the space and growing off the green dowel stems, rising from the flower pots, are a variety of red, yellow and white Fendi bags. A single neon flower emanates from the top of the merchandise, clustered below. A semi-abstract mannequin — dressed in the same colors as the accessories — carries a matching watering can to add some humor to the composition. From across the busy traffic street it is the sizzling flower way over eye level and the impact of the red/yellow/white merchandise that draws the viewer over to more closely study the bags presented in ever-rising tiers.

A

B

Active Sportswear; the clothes to wear when actively engaged in moving, playing — in doing things. It is fun time — it is time for free expression and no repressions. It is time for diagonal lines emphasized in the display composition to suggest movement — action — dynamics.

At Marshall Field's (A) the theme is Stripes — the vertical lines that can be dignified and refined — but the semi-realistic mannequins are definitely not vertical! Arms are akimbo – knees are bent — one figure stands with his legs spread: In all there is a composition of jagged, broken diagonal lines that add vitality and dynamics to the composition which is otherwise neat, orderly — and vertical. The lighting adds a mottled quality to the rear wall which also carries a feeling of energy.

The forms in the Jacobson's display (B) also suggest vitality and movement — from the flying pennants fluttering above to the casual and relaxed draping of the arms in the pockets — the crossed trouser legs and the floating form in shorts. Even the lay-down on the floor of the display space is energized by the draping and shaping of the coordinated garments.

A: Marshall Field's, Chicago, IL
   Jamie Becker, State St. Visual Merchandising Director
   Amy Meadows, Window Manager

B: Jacobson's, Birmingham, MI
   Janice Cecil, Visual Merchandising Director
   Jane Chika, Assistant

C: Macy's, Herald Square, New York, NY

D: Fendi, Fifth Ave., New York, NY

D

C

The body suit is the great all purpose suit for the active life-style and in the Macy's display (C) the surrealistic setting adds to the excitement and enlivens the all black outfit to a new height of fun — even to an armful of fun watches. The watches are so great that they are also used up one leg of the mannequin and more watches are displayed on the "hand" plant growing from the yellow urn in this wacky museum of unreal art.

Just how fashionable can biking be? Well, at Fendi the bikes reach new heights as one climbs the wall of the window. It wouldn't be a Fendi display if it didn't show some of the famous Fendi bags so along with sun glasses and scarves, handbags are tied on to the bikes as colorful accents to the already colorful sportswear mostly in red, yellow and blue. Here, too, the window design is filled with suggested action — with movement "frozen" for the moment — and then illuminated to enhance that moment.

A

B

Purr-fect! Faux Ferocious! The wild at heart are tamed and brought into the fashion scene so whether they be tigers, leopards, zebras or giraffes — no animal is endangered in these fabric reproductions especially since they are all in fun — they are faux and they are in fabric — and patterned to please.

Gucci (A) has upholstered their dress forms with trophies of the hunt; all in black, white and other gold to enhance the presentation of the non-animal skin prints in black and gold. One scarf is framed on the rear wall and another print is used on the jacket of the stylized mannequin on the right. The rich, neutral leather of the Gucci bags is complemented by the faux fur print as they are slung over the shoulders of the forms.

Who would want to change these spots? The background is a blow-up of spots not unlike the smaller ones splattered over the separates in the Escada window (B). Behind the two realistic mannequins in black and white there is a twine covered decorative form draped with an animal print scarf, some "skin" like belts and a bright accent spot of yellow on the scarf draped from the form's hip.

C

A: Gucci, Fifth Ave., New York, NY
James Knight, Corp. Dir. of Visual Presentation

B: Escada, E. 57th St., New York, NY
Gregory Khoury, Display Director

C: Macy's, Herald Square, New York, NY

D: North Beach Leather, Boston, MA
Kristin Lauer, Blue Potatoes, Boston, Designer

D

The trophy bearers — all muscle and brawn — are bringing home the prize catch. The bearers are wearing faux animal skins and the background and floor pads are covered with an ocher and black leopard print. The semi-sheer pull back curtains against the glass that frame the scene are of the same print. Suspended off the raised up brass rods is a Louis XVI chair upholstered in the same fabric and "the prize" is the blonde goddess — the realistic mannequin in the animal print dress. Note that the bag that she carries also is keyed into the animal theme.

Some patterns are just too ferocious to be left to roam around free so North Beach Leather in Boston (D) has put these wild animal prints and the realistic mannequins wearing them behind bars in a simulated zoo setting. The front glass is striped with paint but it could be done with black ribbons or painted wood slats to suggest the cage which, in turn, emphasizes the animal source of the black and other spotted prints on soft and supple leather. The dramatic lighting is right on the penned-up prints.

A

B

A: ZCMI, Salt Lake City, UT
    Mike Stevens, Visual Director
    Diane Call, Designer

B: Charles Jourdan, Trump Tower, New York, NY
    David Griffin, Display Director

C: Jaeger, Madison Ave., New York, NY
    Display by Ideas

D: Saks Fifth Ave., New York, NY
    William Viets, V.P. of Visual Merchandising

More untamed animal prints captured in display set-ups. The *Vogue* fashion show at ZCMI (A) featured the newest and the best and this faux leopard outfit was presented as an elegant example of what was to be shown. A black and white diagonally striped scarf tops the spotted jacket and a white shoulder bag hangs from a decorative metal stand besides the realistic figure. The lighting is mostly deep blues and violets and these lamps are used to wash the walls and floor. A sharp, clear white light identifies and accentuates the jacket. With the giant "*Vogue*" logo on the top of the window, the display becomes a 3-D version of the magazine cover.

What do we call a dog with spots? "Fashionable," especially when these polka dotted pooches are used to further promote the animal print outfit worn by the stylized figure raised up on a build-up of spotted cubes. The white cotton rope leashes lead from the doggies in the window — up front — to the mannequin further back in this open backed window. The overall effect is amusing, fun and definitely eye arresting.

C

D

Graphically Speaking — and these animal prints are graphic as are the giant photo blow-ups in the Jaeger (C) ads that serve as a background for the two black dress forms dressed in the zebra patterned jackets. The large photo directly behind and above the forms shows one of the jackets "in use" — in a life-style setting — while the plaid one adds a bright spot of color to the otherwise black and white composition. The rear wall is covered with black louvered panels and the floor board is finished with an amusing bold pinto pattern.

Another example of zebra stripes elevated to haute couture. The realistic mannequin stands next to a deep red pedestal upon which rests a decorative animal head sculpture which almost looks African. The mannequin's red pocket handkerchief complements the balancing element in the composition, the pedestal, and the tawny setting is washed with a deep gold/amber light except for the mannequin which is picked out with a clear, crisp light.

A

A: ZCMI, Salt Lake City, UT
Mike Stevens, Visual Director
Wendy Krobbe, Designer

B: Macy's, Herald Square, New York, NY

C: Strawbridge & Clothier, Philadelphia, PA
Chris Dixon-Graff, Visual Merchandising Director
The Shooters, Photographers

D: Rori, Caracas, Venezuela
Carlos Brarezonsi, Display Director

B

One of the fun promotions to break in August — to break away from the late summer doldrums and the clearance sales of shorts and swim suits is "Back to School." It means putting an "up" attitude on what many kids think of as a "downer"; putting in color — light and a sense of movement.

ZCMI (A) filled its tall window with boldly colored and oddly shaped forms — hung as mobiles a la Calder in the blacked out window. The young mannequins are dressed up in denims — clean and casual — current and correct. The copy, in yellow gold on the glass reads "An education in Style." The appeal is to the parents who will make the actual purchases but the kids can't complain since these outfits do include colorful high-tops and turnabout baseball caps.

The traditional "cliches" of Back to School get a brand new interpretation at Macy's (B). A simple, angled arch supported by a pair of uprights in viridian green suggests the little old school house and the familiar apple tree is replaced by a birch trunk stabbed with yellow pencils as branches trimmed with green leaves. The base of the birch tree is an oversized sharpened end of a yellow pencil. Big red apples do appear — but as finials atop the kid forms which are totally dressed and accessorized with sweaters and bags, and piles of paper bound up with viridian ribbons serve as elevations for some of the forms. The all-white setting makes everything look crisp, clean and bright — and just right for Back to School.

Though this Strawbridge & Clothier window (C) was designed to announce an Exhibit of Beatrice Potter's work in Philadelphia, it could also serve successfully as a setting for the young children not "going back" — but going off for the very first time to nursery school or kindergarten. The imaginative woodland setting — right out of a fairy tale by way of Disney — the familiar and favorite furry animals — the stories of Peter Rabbit and other tales — they all could create an ideal way of "happily ever after" sending off the very young in their new school outfits.

Going to College is also going back to school and the display at Rori (D) shows young men and women in a setting suggestive of a campus with foam core cut-out and art-worked windows and benches as well as background and floor panels painted in rich, earthy fall colors. The black line artwork on the facades is also repeated on the floor boards to suggest stone and slate walks.

C

D

A

C

B

A: Printemps, Paris, France
   Barbara Heberlein, Display Director
   Jean Colonna & Monica Lomont, Designers

B: Maendler, Munich, Germany
   Peter Rank, Designer

C: Harvey Nichols, London, England
   Mary Portas, Head of Sales Promotion and Visual
       Merchandising

Black is deep, dark and mysterious. Black is smart and sexy — and beautiful. Black when teamed with white is sharp, strong, striking and dynamic. It is the ultimate contrast: The alpha and omega of the lack of color and the overwhelming presence of color. On these pages and those that follow, we show a variety of approaches to the presentation of the always-effective use of no color in contrast with the world of color that surrounds it.

The white mannequin in the black dresses in the Printemps window (A) stand in an ambience of graphic material — thousands upon thousands of sun glasses repeated over and over until it becomes a pattern rather than an object. Superimposed over this "textured" environment are over-scaled eyes and mouth rendered in fashion sketch artwork. It is the scale of the painted features that all but engulf the two figures — and gains the attention for the display.

The designer at Maendler in Munich (B) mixes metaphors — but the result is effective — in black and white.

White fabric cascades down the partial back wall and spreads out like sand dunes in the desert on the window floor. The mannequins wear hats right out of an old foreign legion movie that accentuate the military snap and style of the gold buttoned and gold appliqued tunics and coats. A cold circular moon rises up over the desert as do some unexpected black cacti which are used to balance the figures in this asymmetrical set-up.

Newspapers — especially yesterday's newspapers — are cheap and expendable. They are usually easy to get and they are black and white. Harvey Nichols, on Sloane St. in London (C) featured this arresting three-dimensional sculpture made out of the *London Financial Times* to introduce the black and white "business" suits worn by the realistic mannequins. The theme is "Season's Constructions" and the wonderful giant face constructed of folded newspapers gives way to undulating waves of more newspapers on the floor. The piles of newspapers also become effective elevations for the mannequins.

A

A: Bergdorf Goodman, Fifth Ave., New York, NY
     Richard Currier, V.P. of Visual Presentation

B: Gigi, Munich, Germany
     Peter Rank, Designer

C&D: Henri Bendel, Fifth Ave., New York, NY
     Barbara Putnam, Display Director

B

Ink-blots — splatter and spots — the Rorschach test and Jackson Pollack with a palette limited to black and white. The elegant black gowns are shown in the Bergdorf window (A) in an all-white envelop that is overwhelmed by the splatter and splashes — the blobs and blots — the squiggles and wiggles of black on pristine white. They stand regal and secure while all about them hysteria reigns. It is a sharp contrast of colors as well as temperaments and the madness does get attention.

Gigi of Munich (B) turns the black dress promotion into a black bandage on white display. The background is hung with a white fabric Empire drape and the bits of tree trunks that shoot up throughout the window space are painted stark white then bound and banded to one another with black ribbons that tie up the whole display into a maze of ribbon streamers.

C

You, too, can be the life of the party in a black dress or outfit — with a lamp shade on top. These dress forms not only wear the attention-getting lamp shades but they have been wired so that the shades light up and send out a luminous message. The chair that carries the copy for this Bendel window (C) is shrouded in white muslin which also spills down and spreads out to cover the floor of the window. A two-panel, white screen serves as a partial background for the open back window. Like the Bergdorf "blot" window — there is a dichotomy here: A dignified presentation of fine merchandise that goes slightly awry for attention — but still keeps its sense of value.

There is a real, rip-roaring, chair-tossing party going on in the black and white party clothes window at Bendel (D). Black curtains are pulled back to frame the scene and the gilt and black spindly opera chairs are doing a levitation act in the shallow, open back window. The stylized white mannequins with top hats are wearing mannish-type outfits while the seated figure with the frothy black hat wears a frilly blouse with a long skirt. The floor — to carry out the contrast theme — is checkerboarded in black and white.

D

Black plays against white and white plays against black and only the striped hat puts the two together in the effective Galeries Lafayette window (A) which appears hot and sultry even though the light is clear. The dark sunglasses and the cool, deep shadows make the illuminated areas seem warmer and steamier. Up front, a parade of penguins in black and white move across the white floor to reinforce the "cool" dresses in the "hot" window.

At Bergdorf (B) they are playing with patterns — with white bands outlining black separates, some of which are further embellished with white dots and donuts. The fashion accessories emphasize the black/white combination in dots and stripes and all the bags are black. The central figure wears a black/white polka dotted scarf as a headdress. On the rear wall you are invited to follow the dotted line — to score and cut — to create a pattern of your own. Sunglasses are also accessories of note in this display.

B

C

More play — in black and white. The window at Lord & Taylor (C) has been masked to a new low so that the upper part of the glass is covered with a dropped fringed curtain, thus cutting off from view the whole top of the display space. The interest is down on the floor and the mask focuses the viewer in on the two mannequins stretched out on the white floor. The black and white dotted dominoes standing upright and snaking in and out and around the figures creates the display environment.

Black and white — with myriad strings of mirror chains: Assorted shapes of mirror pieces strung together and liberally hung throughout the Escada (D) space. They catch and reflect the light that is aimed at the realistic mannequin and any slight breeze sets them in motion. The rear black wall is appliqued with large diamonds and squares of mirror which not only catch the light and reflect it onto the small pieces, but give fractured images of the costume on display.

A

A: Galeries Lafayette, E. 57th St., New York, NY

B: Bergdorf Goodman, Fifth Ave., New York, NY
     Richard Currier, V.P. of Visual Presentation

C: Lord & Taylor, Fifth Ave., New York, NY
     William Conard, Director of New York Windows

D: Escada, E. 57th St., New York, NY
     Gregory Khoury, Display Director

Also see: Formals p. 78-81.

D

Black shocked with pink: smart, stylish, and really not so shocking. The white oval frame in the Christian Dior window (A) identifies the store and in this display it frames a giant black and white graphic blow-up of a Dior outfit — in black and white stripes. Up front, on a white dress form is a pinned and draped variation on the pictured theme accented with Dior costume jewelry. The bodice is swathed in hot pink chiffon over the draped black/white striped skirt.

Abstract forms, on the left of the Bendel window (B) wear charcoal gray while the realistic figures wear bright pink jackets over black. Tying them together are the heroic scaled fashion drawings showing a selection of designs and details but it is the strong pink that really draws the viewer over and it is the expert lighting that makes sure it happens.

Fornessetti is the great Italian graphics designer who best expresses himself in black and white and the Fornessetti sun design makes a stellar setting for the elegant black gown on the white dress form and base in the Harvey Nichols window (D). In addition to the print lined coat — a sheer scarf of the luscious lipstick pink is tied around the neck plate of the form and draped down to the right — to the center of the setting.

B

A

D

C

A: **Christian Dior, Fifth Ave., New York, NY**

B: **Bergdorf Goodman, Fifth Ave., New York, NY**
Richard Currier, V.P. of Visual Presentation

C: **Barneys, Seventh Ave., New York, NY**
Simon Doonan, Creative Director

D: **Harvey Nichols, London, England**
Mary Portas, Head of Sales Promotions and
Visual Merchandising

It's all about geometry: of squares and circles — of black and white — of diagonal lines drawn through space and it's the hot pink that enlivens the space and fills it with rich, warm color. The dress forms in Barneys window (C) wear the black/pink suits and both stand on old-fashioned, cast iron, roll-around bases while the props all around are sharp, modern and ultra contemporary. The severity of the angular geometry also makes the simple tailored suits seem "fluid" by comparison.

A

A: Marshall Field's, Chicago, IL
    Jamie Becker, State St. Visual Merchandising Director
    Amy Meadows, Window Manager

B: Lord & Taylor, Fifth Ave., New York, NY
    Alan Petersen, V.P. of Visual Merchandising / Store Design
    William Conard, Director of Fifth Ave. Windows

C: Rori, Caracas, Venezuela
    Carlos Brarezonsi, Display Director

D: Macy's, Herald Square, New York, NY

E: Pilar Rossi, Madison Ave., New York, NY
    Marc Manigault, Display Director

B

C

Black with red: fiery — exciting — exhilarating — and stimulating. The Marshall Field's threesome (A) of realistic mannequins are posed on two levels and unified by the bold, dramatic sweep of red velvet fabric. The uppermost mannequin wears a red coat — to complement the fabric drape — and red light floods over the drape, onto the dark back wall and down onto the floor. The black wrought iron candelabra adds another elegant vertical line to the already vertical composition and the poses of the mannequins.

Black and white outfits are shown at Lord & Taylor (B) on realistic mannequins caught up in the maze of a jungle jim construction of black and white pipes and shelves. The red wall and floor provide the fire that lights up the display and the walls are washed with red light that makes them glow even more. Otherwise, this horizontal composition is quiet and relaxed.

In the Rori display (C) the red jacketed mannequin dominates the window and the red/white/black color scheme is effectively restated in the free flowing and flowery artwork of black lines on white foam board panels highlighted with splashes of brilliant red. The red of the jacket and of the artwork is intensified by the red light that pours over the back wall and spills over onto the foreground.

D

E

It is as simple as, and as basic as, A-B-C, and the alphabet graphic panel spells it all out. It is all about black — about white, and about black and white together in the Macy display (D). It is the red letters that stand out and demand attention — that add a spark to this display. Although they don't in this case, the red letters could spell out a message most effectively. The walls and floors are white and the lighting is neutral; clear — sharp and direct.

This is one tune that the shopper seems never to tire of: black and white combined with red. It is the palette that seems to re-appear each season and is always greeted as something new — and special. It is always fresh and "unexpected" — like an impromptu jazz variation. This musical entertainment was provided by Pilar Rossi (E) and the black and white motif was carried on within the store as well. The red-headed mannequin with the shiny gold saxophone is seated on a simple black chair while yards and yards of musical score sheets unfold off the music stand and drop down to the white marble floor below. A swirl of black music notes and bars is painted on the front glass — to introduce the musical interlude.

A

aura Ashley (B) overcomes the problem of a shallow display window with an open back by having a "curtain" of white satin ribbons up against the front glass. White flowers are caught up with pretty bows on the pendant ribbon streamers and the realistic bride makes her entrance in the center — in the soft spotlight provided for her.

The traditional bride in the traditional gown gets a memory-filled setting at ZCMI (C). The realistic mannequin stands to one side in the soft, diffused light and she is balanced in the composition by the pair of "old" bridal photos in flat, artwork frames and a glass vase in a metal tripod stand brimming over with white gladioli. The background of the window is blacked out and the lettering on the front glass reads "Bridal Bazaar" and proclaims the store's 125th anniversary.

ere comes the bride — and the music swells and the air is filled with the scent of flowers. Bridal means yards and yards of gossamer net and veiling — ribbons and lace — doves and cherubs floating overhead — old fashioned furniture and memorabilia — pipe organs — bridal aisles and bouquets of flowers.

Liberty of London (A) does a turnabout and presents the view most people have of the bride — and her gown — during the ceremony. It is the back of the gown with all its beautiful drapery and detailing. For those who want to see the front and won't wait for the bridal pictures, there is an ornate floral filagree mirror that tells that side of the story. The pearls — purposefully long — hang down in back and the bride's hands are behind her. The wide picture hat all but hides her face. The black vertical lines add a sharp contemporary contrast to all that satin and flowery details.

B

C

A: Liberty of London, London, England
   Paul Muller, Director of Promotions and Visual Presentation

B: Laura Ashley, E. 57th St., New York, NY
   Barbara Klebber, National Visual Merchandising Director

C: ZCMI, Salt Lake City, UT
   Mike Stevens, Visual Merchandising Director
   Celeste Cecchini, Designer

A

B

A: Pilar Rossi, Madison Ave., New York, NY
    Marc Manigault, Display Designer

B: Bergdorf Goodman, Fifth Ave., New York, NY
    Richard Currier, V.P. of Visual Presentation

C&D: Printemps, Paris, France
    Barbara Heberlein, Display Director
    Monica Lomont, Monique Lothon, Designers

Two looks at the more contemporary bride and bridal outfit. At Pilar Rossi (A) though the suit is smart and modern — an old-fashioned loveliness fills in the space. A soft, sheer gold lame drape is partially pulled back to reveal a Venus bust on a white cube pedestal. The bride is wearing a suit — a frilly hat and faux pearls. Behind her — inside the store — the classic theme complements and continues with white columns on the marble floor serving to back up other bridal suggestions. The floor pad in the window is covered with the gold lame fabric. The message: sophisticate classic.

White lace paper doilies are the decorative elements freely used in the Bergdorf bridal window (B). They are lined up against the glass like a scalloped lace edging and they are also scattered about on the floor under the un-traditional bridal outfit of white silk appliqued with dimensional silk flower heads. What really makes this display a stopper is the "wedding cake" hat with veil atop the golden haired wig of the realistic mannequin. A slice has been cut out to reveal the chocolate layers inside the white iced cake topped with yellow and white flower forms. The lighting is warm, soft and gentle — but the humor is also there.

Bride followed bride in the procession in the Printemps windows (C & D) in Paris tied together by yards and yards of floating tulle that filled the long windows sweeping from one bride to the next. The rear wall was pouffed with more clouds of tulle. Caught up in the sweep of draped net were corsages of flowers with ribbon bows and streamers. Occasionally there would be a break in the bridal procession and a bride would be invited to step up a simple cube-like set of steps — into the low slung moline and ribbon trimmed cloud that descends from above. Here the mannequin could show off the back of her gown and the length and details of the train.

C

D

A

B

A&B: Woodward & Lothrop, Washington, DC
          Jack Dorner, V.P. of Visual Merchandising

C&D: ZCMI, Salt Lake City, UT
          Mike Stevens, Display Director
          Sherri Orton, Celeste Cecchini and Dennis Wardle, Designers

hat goes with the bride and groom? The Bridal gifts! It is not unusual as part of a bridal promotion to also devote display space to the exhibition of china, glass, silver and home fashion gift accessories. At ZCMI (C&D) the Bridal Bazaar introduced on p. 37 continues with these two gift displays. Note how the framed pictures of the old-fashioned brides re-appear here. They are overscaled and are set atop a French bureau plat along with some real photos in gift suggestion frames — all emphasizing nostalgia. An arrangement of white lilies appears in the composition to balance some of the china and silver arranged up front in the dark window. The other display shows china and glass on a glass topped contemporary table and several white tulip plants grow in glazed white pots. As a background there is a watery, watercolor painting of a bride — barely perceived in the subtly muted sylvan setting — which complements the cool, aqua/green quality of the up front setting.

The Woodward & Lothrop displays (A&B) on the opposite page combined dimensional props with trompe l'oeil artwork in pink on white to create a series of elegant settings to show off many different gift ideas. Since this is an "at home" wedding their are interiors as well as garden scenes. Some items are shown on the mantle — some on tables — on chairs, benches and even on the floor. By using the many different levels of presentation it was possible for the viewer to absorb the merchandise recommendations in coordinated groups — and then move on to the next group — at a different eye level.

C

D

A

The space above in the Barneys window (B) is devoted to a colorful sun mobile of rotating eyes, nose and mouth surrounded by cut out foam core swirls and curls — some of which are also scattered about on the white floor board. The two semi-realistic kids are animated and fun and go with the swirls and sun used to decorate the space.

Marshall Field's (C) mannequins are also semi-realistic but devoid of make-up or wigs. The theme is — "in Full Bloom" and up front are seed packets lined up next to the curved board base that sweeps up and behind the two carrot-topped kids in almost matching outfits. The third child — far left — is carrying a piece of cloud. To fill in the big upper area of the window a fluffy white cloud cut out of foam board and shaded with strips of blue tissue floats by and a yellow sun peeks out from behind it.

B

Children's wear is usually bright and color filled and thus can just as often be seen as confusing in a display set-up since the garments are smaller in scale and there just isn't enough of the garment to make a clear and direct statement. Also — there is a tendency to fill the space with little mannequins which tends to add to the confusion. A lot of kids crowded together may be realistic but unless they are color coordinated and carefully arranged in levels, they may overkill. Also — since they are smaller and often appear in full size windows — something has to be done in the upper part of the window space to gain attention for the little folks scampering about below.

Laura Ashley (A) fills in that upper space with a handsome and dignified Sale sign. The wooden wheelbarrow filled with flowers and fruits tends to hold the group together in a single composition. The colorful toy rakes and hoes add to the farm and country fresh theme as does the spiral of green hose. The mannequins are stylized and they are compatible in design.

A: **Laura Ashley, E. 57th St., New York, NY**
   Barbara Kleber, National Visual Merchandising Director

B: **Barneys, Manhasset, NY**
   Stephen Johanknecht, Display Manager

C: **Marshall Field's, Chicago, IL**
   Jamie Becker, State St. Window Director
   Amy Meadows, Window Manager

C

A

The Ungaro threesome (A) appear with the most easily recognized classic symbol: the tall, vertical fluted column with or without the Doric, Ionic or Corinthian capital. The Corinthian cap — in large size — serves as a table/elevation in the Saks Fifth Ave. display (B). It is painted white and topped with busts of Beethoven and friend — also white — and also classic. In keeping with it all, the creamy white Empire draping that cascades down to the floor recalls yet another Classic period in art and architecture.

The ornate swirling frames with the Picasso-ish line drawings have to be classic since Marshall Field's (C) has printed on the glass that gray and white suits are classic for the business oriented woman.

As the reader peruses this book, he/she is sure to come upon many more classic examples of "Classic" — which will be pointed out in the text — just in case the reader doesn't spot it.

B

Classic originally referred to the art, architecture and sculpture of the ancient Greeks and Romans but today those "classic" elements are used to define or enhance any item that has an "established degree of excellence" — a pedigree — anything that has proven itself by withstanding time and trends. A Chanel suit is classic — a pump shoe is classic — a simple, well-made and styled suit is classic just as black is basic and navy is classic. Though classic architecture was originally polychromed — painted in bright strong colors — white today means classic; white columns, pedestals, urns, balustrades, sculpture. Ornate baroque and rococo frames and furniture — hardly classic — can still suggest classic especially if painted or finished in white. Sculpture is classic — and paintings in frames can be classic. Old library books with leather bindings are classics — vintage black and white movies from the '30s and '40s are classic. In these three selections we offer only a few of the "classic cliches" the displayperson can use to add "class" to a product display. More are shown under Import on p.104-105.

C

A

rmenegildo Zegna's display (B) relies on an enlargement of a photo showing the structure of a jacket while in the foreground, on a suit form, is an actual jacket — in the making — with basting stitches and all shown along with the "tools of the trade"; scissors, needles, pins, spools of thread and bolts of fabric. The tape measure around the neck plate of the form suggests that the fitting is still going on.

St. John's classic styling (C) is pointed up in the vignette setting which also implies a designer's workshop. On the black back wall there are design sketches pinned up along with swatches of fabric and trimmings. A dress form on a cast iron base is partially papered over with pieces of pattern — partially sewn and somewhat sampled. The realistic mannequin in the stylish suit wears the tape measure around her neck — as though she were in the throes of creating.

B

outure or Couture Fashion means something special — something especially tailored and fitted — made to order. It means NOT run-of-the-mill or mass produced — but does mean unique. Couture suggests hand processes — a designer — yards of fabric — dress forms — tape measures — patterns — sketches — drawing boards — studios — workshops — ateliers. Couture — if Haute enough — can also be boiserie, Louis XV and Louis XVI fauteuils and bergeres, crystal chandeliers, white tables with bandied legs weighted down with gilt and bronze d'Or.

Here are three displays that take the "fine tailoring" approach to fashion. The Barneys display (A) fills the display space with dress forms, patterns and a pin-up board with "work in progress" — all to support the idea of a fashion atelier. The three stylized mannequins wear basic, classic outfits in black and white.

A: **Barneys, Seventh Ave., New York, NY**
    Simon Doonan, Creative Director

B: **Ermenegildo Zegna, Fifth Ave., New York, N**

C: **St. John, Fifth Ave., New York, NY**
    Kelly Gray, V.P. Creative Director

C

Calvin Klein on 2

A

B

C

D

Cruise and Resort wear usually makes its window debut while we are bundled up in our wintery wear. Here a stuffed crocodile (or alligator) slithers across the yellow/gold straw mat on the floor of the Saks Fifth Ave. window (A) completely ignoring the not-to-be-ignored mannequin in the white outfit. Clusters of natural bamboo rods topped with strands of raffia suggest a bamboo forest and the ocher colored wall is left in shadows. A yellow light washes over the bamboo and the reptile on the floor while a white light enhances the figure's position in the composition.

Bamboo and raffia again appear — with a difference. In the Laura Ashley window (B) the mood is lighter — gayer and more playful as some wooden monkeys swing and scamper back and forth amid the headless forms in their casual white Resort wear.

A more sophisticated approach which hints at Cruisin' but avoids the usual "cliches." The Bergdorf window (C) creates a "jungle" out of sheets of kraft paper woven together — entwined and enmeshed — with strings of natural twine to complement these cruise suits in creamy white — topped with straw hats. A cool light chills the rear wall while warm light enhances the clothes up front.

A completely different approach to warm white neutrals for Cruise/Resort wear: cracked crockery! Plates are cracked, smashed or just chipped and then partially reassembled on the back wall panel to make a most attention-getting display. More of the crockery is scattered about on the white floor of Barneys window (D). The pale yellow and gold colors of suits go well with the subtle background color of the crockery panel.

A: **Saks Fifth Ave., New York, NY**
William Viets, V.P. of Visual Merchandising

B: **Laura Ashley, E. 57th St., New York, NY**
Barbara Kleber, National Visual Merchandising Director

C: **Bergdorf Goodman, Fifth Ave., New York, NY**
Richard Currier, V.P. of Visual Presentation

D: **Barneys, Seventh Ave., New York, NY**
Simon Doonan, Sr. V.P., Advertising/Display

A

B

One of the truly bright spots in the Cruise/Resort scene is usually fresh and flowery pink. It is a color that sings out on the bleakest days and gladdens the heart. Here are some cruise settings featuring that happy color.

Natural terra cotta ceramic jugs and urns serve as the props for this rich and vibrant pink/red outfit. The Saks Fifth Ave. window (A) is filled with deep amber light that magically turns the jugs to rich gold and the clear lights on the realistic red headed mannequin makes the hot pink shirred top jump out from the earth colored setting.

A fantasy tree of fabric palm fronds, raffia and a black pole to support it all makes a complementary background for the pink dress in the foreground. The "tree" also acts to separate the display from the rest of the store which is just beyond it. A hot yellow light provides the strong feeling of sunshine in this Hirshleifer display (B) and makes the sunglasses an absolute must. On the floor a snakey sun is sketched to follow through on the resort theme.

D

A: **Saks Fifth Ave., New York, NY**
   William Viets, V.P. of Visual Merchandising

B: **Hirshleifer's, Manhasset, NY**
   Display by Ideas

C: **Laura Ashley, E. 57th St., New York, NY**
   Barbara Kleber, National Visual Merchandising Director

D: **Lord & Taylor, Fifth Ave., New York, NY**
   William Conard, Director of New York Windows

C

Assorted colored sea horses float in the narrow Laura Ashley window (C) and they are color coordinated to go with the coral/pink top and the print separates that combine the coral with the soft green and yellow. The floor pad is covered in yellow.

Sunny and stunning in the pink! At Lord & Taylor (D) thin pliable bamboo rods are woven in and out to create an open grid within the metal frame that holds it. Natural colored gravel is on the floor and the walls are mottled and textured in yellow and ocher. A cut-out sun is applied over the wall and lit from behind. The merchandise features print separates with hot pink jackets and dress. The lighting is designed to bring out the sunny attitude of the Cruise setting. For more Pink — see p. 32-33 and p. 82-83.

B

The bright, strong and brilliant colors of Cruise. The Macy's background (A) is accomplished with torn pieces of seamless paper. The sky is bright yellow — the water is turquoise, and a giant starfish torn out of royal blue paper is superimposed between. The all-important, fun fashion accessories are displayed with the color-filled outfits.

Cruise means travel — and though the Leaning Tower of Pisa is land-locked, these pink, yellow and blue outfits are ready to board and be off. The Bergdorf display (B) uses a cool, neutral background to offset the vibrant colors of the merchandise and the tilted Tower lends interest as well as a touch of foreign intrigue.

C

A: Macy's, Herald Square, New York, NY

B: Bergdorf Goodman, Fifth Ave., New York, NY
   Richard Currier, V.P. of Visual Presentation

C: Escada, E. 57th St., New York, NY

D: Fendi, Fifth Ave., New York, NY

E: Rori, Caracas, Venezuela
   Carlos Brarezonsi, Display Director

E

E is for Escada (C) and Escada is ready to take off. The giant dimensional letter is tied up with white cotton roping and the swim suited mannequin has all her accessories at hand in the cool, all-white setting.

Fendi (D) takes on Cruise with a flourish. The semi-abstracts stand about beneath a towering palm tree in a hot and sultry setting. The floor is strewn with coconuts and a colorful selection of Fendi bags climb up the burlap wrapped tree trunk — from the floor up to the foliage — snaking their way into the viewer's field of vision.

Ship ahoy! And they are off and away at Rori's (E) in a rowboat with a striped sail and a pinwheel yellow and red sun spirals above the rich blue sky background. It is all fun and frolic; strong, fresh colors — simple foam board constructions — bold patterns and an assortment of base-ball caps of many colors to tie it all together. For continuity the cotton roping stretches from unit to unit.

D

A

B

ruising means going to sea — and go to sea means going "nautical" — and what is more nautical than navy blue — white — splashes of red — stripes — brass buttons — pennants and flags — sailors and sails and miles of white roping.

At Ralph Lauren-Polo (A) it is all about sailing and things nautical clutter up the prop filled space which features the traditional navy brass buttoned blazer and other yachting outfits. The yellow canvas sail serves as a sunny background and a white sea-going duffle bag hangs down from it. Stenciled on the glass is the American flag and reference to the America's Cup races — the ultimate in gentlemanly sailing and racing.

The stylized ladies in the Sonia Rykiel display (B) are showing off their white and navy outfits accented with brass chains. Semaphoring pennants cut diagonally across the white space adding color, movement and the feeling of sea breezes. The floor pad is covered with a navy and white striped fabric and laid out on it are a selection of fashion accessories and coordinates.

Down to the sea in blue, white and nautical stripes. A piece of white muslin suggests a sail as it also separates the mannequin, up front, from the store behind. White cotton roping hangs down from the top of the "sail" to become wrapped around the anchor stay and then continues on to the mannequin's hand in the Elizabeth Arden display (C). The eye follows the route of the rope — and takes in all that the display designer meant to show off. A natural wood plank platform finishes off this nautical vignette.

Red, white and blue — stripes and solids — and brass buttons; that's what nautical and cruising is all about. The ambience is all white and free standing panels (actually supported by the overhead framework) of red and navy are framed in gold and be-decked with dimensional over-sized brass buttons. At Jordan Marsh (D) they really know how to salute a season.

For more Navy see p. 154.

D

C

A: **Ralph Lauren-Polo, Madison Ave., New York, NY**

B: **Sonia Rykiel, Madison Ave., New York, NY**
   Marc Manigault, Display Design

C: **Elizabeth Arden, Fifth Ave., New York, NY**
   Noel MacFetrich, Display Director

D: **Jordan Marsh, Boston, MA**
   Joe Conti, V.P. of Visual Merchandising

A

B

N avy — always right for Cruise wear teams up beautifully with stripes — with white and with cheerful yellow for a splash of sunshine.

In the subdued light of the Gucci window (A) it is possible to discern the male mannequin wearing navy, white and striped sportswear separates. The floor pad is white with a giant conch shell drawn on it in yellow and pin pricks of light pick out the real large conch shells that are used to prop this seafaring set-up.

At Ferragamo (B) Cruise means going tropical and what is more tropical and bright yellow than bananas? Giant foam core cut out bananas are supported by bamboo rods and tied up with natural raffia to provide a background for the navy and white separates shown on the black abstract mannequins that all but disappear into the black background. Along with the shoes in navy and white highlighted on the floor is a lovely bunch of bananas — life-size. There is no slip-up here!

et the sun shine in at Aquascutum (C). The sports separates are navy, white and yellow and the vignette setting suggests a dock — a boat mooring — a fishing shack in Key West. A simple construction of planks and 1x2 lumber becomes the dock and railing. A louvered panel serves as the side of the shack and cardboard tubes — wrapped with heavy cotton roping are the pilings in the water. Everything has been painted white except the piles of sand on the floor which are almost white. A bright yellow blob of light stains the louvered panel and spreads out over some of the mannequins — flooding them with glorious sunlight.

C

A: Gucci, Fifth Ave., New York, NY
   James Knight, Corp. Director of Visual Presentation

B: Ferragamo, E. 56th St., New York, NY
   Gilbert Vanderweide, Display Director

C: Aquascutum, Fifth Ave., New York, NY
   Displays by Ideas

D: Gucci, Fifth Ave., New York, NY
   James Knight, Corp. Director of Visual Presentation

D

A

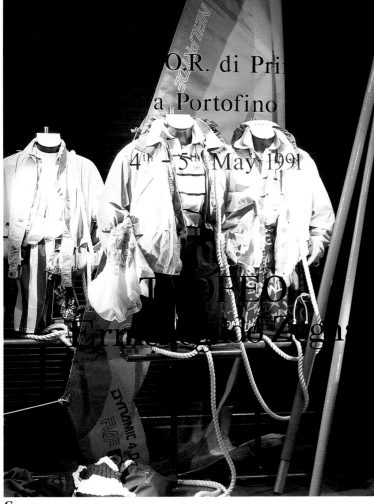

C

B

Sea and sun fashions for the boys in sharp, clear colors. Piped aboard at Macy's (A) are these headless forms dressed to the nines in Polo fashions. What makes the colors sing out is the all whitewashed setting: from the walls and floor — the panelled dado — the applied strips of 1x4 that holds the life jackets and buoys and such — and, of course, the funnel that shares the spotlight with the forms and really sets the time and place for the sportswear.

The "invisible man" in the Saks Fifth Ave. window (B) is charting his course, of course, in all the right clothes with coordinated alternatives laid out on the floor — should he decide to make a change or detour. Seagoing flags are unfurled on a rope that is held taut in the foreground and a rod equipped with brass hooks carries an extra jacket for the trip. The "illusion" of the man is very well executed and is an attention getting device in itself.

Sails, oars, and yards of cotton roping turn these three casually rigged suit forms at Zegna (C) into sea-going sailors. The analogous color scheme runs the gamut from yellow to green to blue; cool water, clear skies and a dollop of sun above. The white rope runs rampant in and out and around the composition — tying it all up and when the rope drops down to the floor of the window it leads the viewer to the additional merchandise displayed there.

WATERWAYS

D

A: **Macy's, Herald Square, New York, NY**

B: **Saks Fifth Ave., New York, NY**
   Matt Reed, Mens Window Manager

C: **Ermenegildo Zegna, Fifth Ave., New York, NY**

D: **Woodward & Lothrop, Washington, DC**
   Jack Dorner, Vice President of Visual Merchandising

Waterways is the tag-line for the Woodward & Lothrop window (D). Seafarers in white, yellow, red and blue are beautifully arranged on a composition of white cubes of different heights. Balancing the forms on the cubes is an intricately cut-out foam board panel painted rich blue which is a lacework of waves and seashells. The rear wall and floor of the window are white and while a warm light enhances the colors of the garments, a cool blue light deepens the color of the cut-out panel and the wall behind it.

A

ed and white gingham goes wild in this Denim display at Daffy's (B). The fanciful gingham covered props and mannequins were executed in conjunction with a class of display students at the Fashion Institute of Technology in New York and the result is startling and a shopper stopper. The kid's kite is caught in the tree and tablecloth covered clouds drift across the sharp blue sky. The floor is covered with green grass matting.

Standing on the corner and watching the girls go by and hoping one will stop are these teenagers in the Macy's, San Francisco window (C). The city-scape — in contrast to the country landscapes is suggested by the high-tech materials — the bolts, "metal clad columns" — the billboards and the rusty patina on most surfaces. Backwards baseball caps are the accessories of choice in the subdued lighting of the urban setting.

A: **Lord & Taylor, Fifth Ave., New York, NY**
    William Conard, Director New York Windows

B: **Daffy's, Fifth Ave., New York, NY**
    Mary Costantini, Display Director

C: **Macy's, San Francisco, CA**

he All-American fabric — with the French name — DENIM. The universal color that seems to go with about everything — that goes anywhere at any time and is frequently teamed up with red and white to show off its Yankee Doodle heritage. Whether it is down on the farm or across the prairies teamed up with cotton bandanas and straw hats — in factories and workshops or just for standing around the corner and watching the world go by — it can be done in denims.

Lord & Taylor (A) goes down to the farm with this modern milkmaid in her denim colored dress which is accented with the traditional and homey, red and white checkered cloth. She sits atop the cut-out and dimensionalized cow mottled in blue and in the foreground — on the straw strewn floor — a rustic milking stool becomes an elevation for a build up of milk bottles and an "antique" wire egg container. More red and white cloth highlights this presentation.

B

C

A

B

C

A&B: Willowbrook Mall, Wayne, NJ
       Glenn Sokoli, Display

C: White Marsh Mall, White Marsh, MD
     Jarri Lugo, Creative Director

Mall management — looking for "universal themes" where the individual retailers can contribute merchandise to be shown as part of a joint display effort and can be credited for their participation — can't go wrong with Denim — and especially denim combined with red and white and smacking of an American celebration.

At the Willowbrook Mall, the concept was a "Go West" look and denim became the great common denominator. The designer combined the denim and denim-colored merchandise with red/white and blue/white ginghams and checks — with printed cotton bandanas and straw hats. For propping the large display stages (A&B) weathered wood boarding, wagon wheels, ropes and greenery were used. Each fully accessorized mannequin was "credited" with a card at the base of the figure; who provided what part or parts of the above outfit.

The White Marsh Mall (C) — just outside of Baltimore, MD, combined denims and blue clothes with red and white accessories to tell a Red/White/Blue, bang-up, cracker jack, All-American story. Existing supporting columns were wrapped with boldly striped bunting and they became the beacons — reaching across the mall to all levels — calling the shoppers to come over and see the mass joint effort on view on the island stages surrounded by "moats" filled with water. The design staff created the unifying red tams that were worn by the female mannequins, and the white tennis shoes — which were another constant — were laced with sassy red bows.

For more Denim ideas see Western on p. 220 , and there are more Mall Presentations on p. 120-125.

A

A: Saks Fifth Ave., New York, NY
    William Viets, V.P. of Visual Merchandising

B: Fendi, Fifth Ave., New York, NY

C: Lord & Taylor, Fifth Ave., New York, NY
    Alan Petersen, V.P. of Visual Merchandising/Store Desig
    William Conard, Director of New York Windows

B

Easter is a spring presentation and most stores have been bypassing the traditional Easter windows with lilies, parades, and bonnets in favor of more non-sectarian displays which say Spring; heavy on tulips in pots, park benches, budding branches, and bits of architecture combined with climbing ivy, grass and gravel. But to children of all ages — Easter is still the Easter bunny, yellow chicks, colored and patterned eggs — and here are some contemporary adaptations of these familiar motifs.

Growing out of giant terra cotta urns are flower-splashed print dresses. They rise out of the shredded green excelsior (another Easter cliche) which spills over on to the ground where it becomes the "grass." All of the old familiars are here: the pastel colored rabbits — the giant foil covered "chocolate" eggs — and the ivy crawling up and entwining about the wire framed gazebo that frames the little girl dresses in the Saks Fifth Ave. window (A). More excelsior and plastic eggs sit atop the neck plates of the forms. The rear wall is tinted with spring green light and the dresses are picked out in pale pink light.

C

Oversized is a small way to describe the wonderful eggs in the Fendi window (B). Just how over-scaled they are can be seen by comparing them with the single handbag sitting up front next to the copy card. These monster mache eggs are hand painted with scenes and with the art and architecture of Italy — as a special tribute to the Italian designers and artisans who create the Fendi products — and to the Italian heritage of the firm. Each piece of artwork is identified with the name of the artist. This is a great idea for an institutional Easter display where artists and artisans can be acknowledged.

Lord & Taylor (C) has gone back to the farm — again — to come up with a display for these spring bonnets. Chickens with distinct personalities and pizazz are setting on straw nests and producing the pastel colored eggs for the holiday. Mixed in with this barnyard madness are wide brimmed straw hats lavishly a-bloom with spring blossoms, ribbons and bows — just waiting to hatch and latch on to a smart Easter outfit. The streaked and stroked yellow/ocher background gets a treatment of golden light while sharp lights help to pick out the feath-ered hens from the flowered hats.

A

A: **Harvey Nichols, London, England**
Mary Portas, Head of Sales Promotion
and Visual Merchandising

B: **Lord & Taylor, Fifth Ave., New York, N**
William Conard, Director of Fifth Ave.
Windows

C: **Ann Taylor, E. 57th St., New York, NY**

D: **ZCMI, Salt Lake City, UT**
Mike Stevens, Display Director
Diane Call, Designer

B

C

GLAMOUR

Show, September 12
ZCMI Mall, center court
Tickets available in our Credit Office

D

Fall is the time for nature — for things natural and rich in texture — for bare, crinkly and twisted branches, for pebbles and stones, bark and brown crumpled paper, fallen leaves, golden light and earthy colors.

A woven twig fence spans across the Harvey Nichols window (A) and growing out behind it is a wonderfully twisted and tortured bunch of twigs that reach up to snare and snaggle a wayward umbrella. Printed gold and blue/green tartan fabrics wend their way through the highly textured space and the expert lighting casts shadows of the branches onto the white floor of the window.

Birch tree trunks and leafless bushes provide a skeletal, webbed setting for the russet and brown leather garments in the Lord & Taylor display (B). The lighting is low keyed — rich, deep and very atmospheric.

The trees in the Ann Taylor display (C) have lost their leaves — but not their shapes and thus not all is lost. Gathered up on the floor at the feet of the stylized mannequin deep green and mulberry colored leaves and a few leaves have been tacked back onto the spindly branches. The floor is laid with natural wood planks to add another natural texture to the set-up.

ZCMI (D) introduces their Glamour Fall Show with a fabulous background made up of inexpensive, easy-to-get brown kraft wrapping paper; crinkled and scrunched up — full of deep shadows and raised planes that catch the amber light that suffuses the space. The mannequin in the pumpkin colored jacket sits in an art deco-inspired, wire frame chair — smooth and slick in contrast to the crumpled look behind her.

A

A: **Ferragamo, E. 56th St., New York, NY**
    Gilbert Vanderweide, Display Director

B: **Burberry's, E. 57th St., New York, NY**
    Michael Stewart, Display Director

C: **Fendi, Fifth Ave., New York, NY**

D: **St. John's, Fifth Ave., New York, NY**
    Kelly Gray, V.P. Creative Director

Fall is harvest time — the time when the earth yields up a bounty of fruits and vegetables — apples, pears, fat and luscious grapes dangling from green to red and on to purple — cornucopias spilling over with foliage and pumpkins and gourds growing to sizes of great importance. Wheat and corn flourish, and everywhere we see yellows, golds, ochers, oranges, and the red and purples.

At Ferragamo (A) the black stylized figures are harvesting the fashionable earth colors as well as the fruits. A rustic rod supports two baskets piled high with oranges and the mannequin carries that prop while another seems to be raking in more oranges to collect in the provincial baskets. The diagonal slash of orange colored wall behind unifies the orange, gold and russet colors of the garments in the deep, autumnal sunset lighting of the window.

A diagonal of rough, raw wood planking sprouts some frizzled and frazzled twigs in the Burberry window (B) and the spot picks out the pile of amber colored leaves on the floor which recalls the color of the garments in the presentation. Layered suitforms carry off the fashions with aplomb as they are highlighted in the dramatically illuminated space.

B

C

Big — almost bare branches span across the high Fendi window (C) creating an arch for the stylized mannequin beneath it with her tumble of wonderfully rich, natural colored leather bags. The window is a blaze of yellows, oranges and reds — created by the lighting on the wood veneered walls. Hanging off the branches are golden apples plus some gold colored chains, ear clips and necklaces. Some of the golden apples have fallen to the ground and a pin prick of light illuminates them in radiant light.

The Cinderella in the St. John's (D) display could have her choice of carriages to take her to the ball. She is already dressed for the gala and there are more than enough fat pumpkins around to do the trick. It may not be Halloween and it certainly isn't a trick — but this black window featuring a gold enriched black dress is definitely an October treat. The subdued lighting further enhances the gilt pattern on the front of the dress.

A: **Maendler, Munich, Germany**
   Peter Rank Design

B: **Gigi, Munich, Germany**
   Peter Rank Design

C: **The Avenue, New York, NY**
   Gayle Massia, Display Director

D: **Kaufmann's, Pittsburgh, PA**
   David Knouse, V.P. of Visual Merchandising

A

B

C

D

Textures do make a difference and fall displays are usually filled with rough rather than smooth tex tures — to complement the wools and surfaced fabrics of the season. Raw wood planking makes an urban style wall behind the ladies in the Maendler display (A) while old, weathered wooden spools probably rolled in off the street where they were abandoned add yet another feeling to the composition. An open, slatted platform made of planks of wood raise the mannequins off the gravel covered floor and the overhead lighting plays up the subtle browns, taupes, and rust colored outfits.

For a more sophisticated approach, the Gigi window (B) offers two mannequins in red costumes set in a helter skelter construction of 1x3 lumber finished with gold leaf against a rear wall also layered in gold. The clever construction — full of action — diagonal lines cutting back and forth through the space — contrasts with the elegant vertical poses of the mannequins. By playing up the shine and glitter of the gold lumber, the viewer gets to see the two figures in the middle of an intricate frame/arch.

More rough textures appear in The Avenue (C) where pieces of tree trunks seem to rise up only to disappear behind the top valance of the not-very-tall window. Assorted bark covered logs serve as seats and risers — as well as add to the outdoors setting. Dried leaves are liberally scattered about on the floor and some furry woodland denizens appear to put the "wild" in "wilderness." The sky blue background tends to open up the display space and make more of it.

In a more "interior" manner; the fall feeling is captured in the wire work and foliage arrangement used by Kaufmann's (D) to introduce the new Ann Klein collection for fall. The setting is almost formal — and like a fashion show stage — with the wire planters to each side and a low wire frame table behind, center. The basket in the foreground and the positioning of the mannequin "break" the symmetry just enough to reinforce the casual message of the outfit.

Sure as there is a third Sunday in June — there will be a Father's Day, and aside from all the jokes about ties given and not worn — shirts too small, and slippers too large, it is a day to celebrate "The Man of the Year" — "That Grand Old Guy" — "The Top Man on the Family Totem Pole." Whether it is nostalgia, humor, a love of sports or hobby, there is always an approach that also allows for merchandise presentation.

Barneys (A/B/D) turns its main windows over to the celebration of the myriad kinds of fathers — and the myriad styles and fashions that the store carries to appeal to all those different kinds of Dads. In a 3-D collage of bits and pieces of graphics, of architectural elements, of photos and gravures of fathers of days of yore in assorted frames — the designers created arresting compositions — heavily layered and textured — that beckoned to the passerby — inviting him/her to come closer to study the many marvelous pieces assembled in each setting — along with the appropriate gift merchandise. In one (A) a semi-realistic figure is surrounded by tubes and tires, by stop and danger signs, "men at work" markers, and even a striped barrier that had been broken through. In another (B) the sportswear is inundated by the assorted memorabilia including western wear and cowboy gear, guitars, steer horns, stuffed deer heads and antlers, an old license plate — from a Western state, of course, and trout too long out of water.

A

B

D

E

C

acy's (C) made a great big bow to the All-Ameri
can sport of baseball in its tribute to the greatest
sport of them all — Dad. The theme was "take
me out to the ball game" and as part of the outfit shown, the
special "accessory" was a catcher's body shield which
appeared under blazers, sports jackets and windbreakers
along with other sports equipment and paraphernalia. To
further the theme and create a follow-through look in the
shadow boxes that followed this one, baseball bats were
line up along the rear wall.

Rori (E) showed a large cut-out caricature of Dad —
with shirt and tie flying in the wind — all flat and decora-
tively rendered. Pinned on to the panel was an assortment
of shirts and ties — gift ideas for Dad — a man on the run.

A/B/D: **Barneys, Seventh Ave., New York, NY**
Simon Doonan, Sr. V.P. Advertising/Display
Steven Johanknecht, Assistant V.P., Display Director

C: **Macy's, Herald Square, New York, NY**
Steven Kornachek, V.P. of Visual Merchandising

E: **Rori, Caracas, Venezuela**
Carlos Brarezonsi, Display Director

B

Dad as a cartoon character? Dad can take a joke and is often the joke on the receiving end of a Father's Day display because he can take it — he's a great, good sport.

Macy's (A) offers a variety of cartoony heads for Dad on his day and the heads are sketched in black on the white rear wall and all over the white floor. Because Dad can be anyone — the headless forms were used so that any head would do while the kid figure has a naive '30s quality. Additional gift suggestions in full vibrant color are displayed on the shelf unit against the wall.

A: **Macy's, Herald Square, New York, NY**
   Steven Kornachek, V.P. of Visual Merchandising

B: **Bergdorf Goodman, Fifth Ave., New York, NY**
   Richard Currier, V.P. of Visual Presentation
   George Shimko, Dir. of Mens Store Display

C: **Saks Fifth Ave., New York, NY**
   William Viets, V.P. of Visual Merchandising

C

A much more delicate and sensitive approach to the multi-faceted Dad of the '90s is seen in the Bergdorf Store for Men (B) where the layered suit form is overstocked with all sorts of recommendations; shirts, ties, belts and more with the overflow set up on the floor near the shoes. It is the graphic in the background that really tells the Father's Day story: a little hand reaching out for and grasping Dad's finger — for safety, assurance, and for the feeling that all will be well.

Humor and sensitivity are combined in the Saks Fifth Ave. display (C). A kid mannequin wearing Dad's shirt, sweater and tie (gift ideas) is seated atop some brand new luggage (another gift suggestion) and seems sort of upset because Dad's clothes are too big for him. On the white wall there are markings indicating the child's progress in growing up — but he still isn't big enough! A short story captured in a very well done display.

A

B

C

A: **Saks Fifth Ave., New York, NY**
   William Viets, V.P. of Visual Merchandising
   Matt Reed, Men's Wear

B: **Lord & Taylor, Fifth Ave., New York, NY**
   Alan Petersen, V.P. of Visual Merchandising/Store Design

C: **Ermenegildo Zegna, Fifth Ave., New York, NY**

D: **Lazoff's, Puerto Rico**
   Frank Caballero, Display Designer
   Photo: Mark Bacon

Making a list and checking it twice — or more times. A great reminder that Father's Day is almost here: The giant clipboard on the rear wall offers some basic gift ideas and the yellow check marks become a symbol that is repeated in the window at Lazoff's (D) as well as inside the store — to keep the message going on the selling floor where the merchandise is available. Actual clipboards are used to show off some shirts while others are highlighted by the attention-getting yellow check marks. The simple wood veneered two-level platform carries a lay down of other gift ideas that can also be checked out or checked off.

In a different mood, Saks Fifth Ave. (A) makes effective use of the tilted cheval mirror to replay the lay down of fashion accessories on the piled up luggage. In a soft light — on the rear wall is a cartoon drawing of a pipe-smoking Dad or "the old man" — the man whose day is being celebrated and for whom the merchandise is being arranged.

Zegna (C) salutes the day by unfurling dozens of ties in the green grass matted window. The wind is blowing and there is a tie in someone's future. It takes a lot of time, effort and talent to create this seemingly simple display — but the end result is worth it.

D

Father's Day ties in so conveniently with early summer sportswear promotions and at Lord & Taylor (B) they tie the two together to show off some fun-in-the-sun relaxin' sportswear — for the man who should take it easy. A planked boardwalk elevates the headless forms and the rolls of dune fencing. Since L&T

has an elevator window — the floor level can be brought way down below street level — the figure on the far right is descending down to the beach which is under the board-walk. A sun on the rear wall is all it takes to finish off the outdoors setting.

A

A: **Lord & Taylor, Fifth Ave., New York, NY**
   Alan Petersen, V.P. of Visual Merchandising
   William Conard, Director of New York Windows

B: **Saks Fifth Ave., New York, NY**
   William Viets, V.P. of Visual Merchandising

C: **Pilar Rossi, Madison Ave., New York, NY**
   Marc Manigault, Display Designer

D: **Barneys, Seventh Ave., New York, NY**
   Simon Doonan, Sr. V.P. Advertising/Display

Formal wear is usually elegant, refined and definitely top drawer. It calls for settings that enhance the garment — that suggests the time and place of the festivity or gala — that creates a mood that enriches the moment — or provides the setting of a dream come true.

Lord & Taylor (A) turns the mannequin around so that the detailing of the back of the dress gets the shopper's attention. The mannequin is stretched out on a French provincial bureau plat with an electrified candelabra as the only other accent prop. The rear wall is marked off in diamond shapes fashioned from satin and shiny black squares that gently reflect a glimmering of what is happening up front. The mannequin holds a single white calla lily — a real classy touch.

In our selection on Classics (see p. 44-45) we mentioned the column and here it is beautifully illustrated at Saks Fifth Ave. (B). The tall, elegant vertical line of the fluted column adds stature and a sense of refinement to the already handsome gowns in basic black. The columns are finished in gold leaf and then burnished with the red and amber lighting. The presentation is low keyed, dramatic and rich — as is the L&T just viewed.

B

D

C

Heavenly is the harp and this beautiful harp carved, embossed and golden becomes the mood setting prop in the Pilar Rossi display (C). It endows the small, open back window with a rich, classic aura that also enhances the beautiful ball gown. As an extra dollop on top: A music staff is painted in gold and black across the front glass along with gold leaf filled musical notes to mark the score. Simple and simply elegant.

Light up the night and this black gown is joined with several very unusual, sculpted lighting fixtures — on wheels with their wires dragging across the white floor of the window. The uniqueness of the lamps — their sculptural quality — attract the viewer's attention and the fine composition brings it all back to the stylized figure in black. Part of the rear wall is drenched in deep blue light which also creates the wonderful shadows on the wall behind the lamps.

A

A&B: Bergdorf Goodman, Fifth Ave., New York, NY
Richard Currier, V.P. of Visual Presentation

C: Hirshleifer's, Manhasset, NY
Displays by Ideas

D: Elizabeth Arden, Fifth Ave., New York, NY
Noel MacFetrich, Display Director

Think Formal: think Black — as we have shown — and also think White. The dance goes on in the Bergdorf window (A) where a Braque-like circle of dancers — in black and white — sets the scene. One of the dancers is filled in with red and stands out — accentuating the single white gown from the two black ones on view. Though the white gown stands out from the contrasting background it takes the fine lighting to define the black gowns in the dark setting. In the display (B) we have a study in contrasts on textures rather than colors. The soft, wispy gown is purposefully contrasted with the rough textured tree trunk that serves as a pedestal for the realistic mannequin and the maze of forsythia branches that spread out behind the figure is about to sprout some yellow/green buds that will flower. The rear wall is tinted with a pale green light while a whisper of yellow light stains the white gown to a creamy loveliness.

B

D

C

The "abstract sculpture," a la Dubuffet, is black, white and blue and adds a contemporary/classic smartness to the gown with the feather tipped skirt and white bodice bow. The stylized mannequin — finished also in white — is carefully accessorized and the darkness behind allows her to step forward for better viewing in the soft illumination. The darker and deeper the background — the less light it requires to make an accentuating statement up front.

Like the Hirshleifer display just mentioned (C), the Elizabeth Arden window (D) also uses a sharp black background to contrast with the white gown lavishly trimmed with gold. This open back window relies on a black panel covered with a pattern of tumbling numbers to block the view into the store — somewhat. This was a New Year's Eve display and the numbers marked the passing of the old year as the dissolve and faded away onto the floor.

A

B

Pink is pretty — pink is feminine — pink can be pale and pastel — or it can be hot and sensuous. Here are some examples of how pink formal wear has been shown: different attitudes for different types and styles of gowns.

Bendel (A) plays Musical Chairs with gold ballroom chairs for their fabulous collection of pink patterned party dresses while Hirshleifer (B) does something with chairs that is completely different. These chairs seem to be carved out of classic sculptures and they are finished in gold and cyclamen pink. The mannequin in the black and white striped dress uses her chair as a way to get up in the setting while the one in hot pink with the striking ostrich boa stands beside her on the floor pad covered with the small black/white checkerboard pattern. Though the window is open backed, the bulk of the chairs and the strong up front lighting diminishes the effect of the store's interior on the display space.

In the Hirshleifer display (C), a "mirrored" panel in an artwork frame is used as part of the illusion and the viewer on the street sees over and over again the front then the back — on to infinity of the pink satin dress in all its grandeur. The "trick" is to use a pair of mannequins posed and dressed in exactly the same way — with one looking into the "mirror" and the other being "the mirror image." A mylar panel is placed on the rear wall — not inside the frame — and it will reflect over and over again the two mannequins. To complete the dramatic presentation a pair of dark velvet drapes hang down at either side — against the front glass like a mask or proscenium that encompasses and concentrates the action in the window.

The lady in the pink brocade suit is about to step out for a night on the town and that town is visible beyond her pink mullioned window where she sits on a window seat. Flowers in terra cotta planters and some framed graphics complete the pink-on-pink vignette at Saks Fifth Ave. (D).

Also see p. 50.

D

C

A: **Henri Bendel, Fifth Ave., New York, NY**
   Barbara Kleber, Display Director

B&C: **Hirshleifers, Manhasset, NY**
   Displays by Ideas

D: **Saks Fifth Ave., New York, NY**
   William Viets, V.P. of Visual Merchandising

A&B: **Lord & Taylor, Fifth Ave., New York, NY**
Alan Petersen, V.P. of Visual Merchandising/Store Design
William Conard, Director New York Windows

C: **Henri Bendel, Fifth Ave., New York, NY**
Barbara Putnam, Display Director

D: **ZCMI, Salt Lake City, UT**
Mike Stevens, Display Director
Celeste Cecchini, Designer

B

A

C

Special events — special promotions — special affairs and premiers call for Formal wear and Formals are often shown in conjunction with the opening of the opera season — the arrival of a ballet company — the symphony series — a benefit performance — a charity gala.

To celebrate the 100th anniversary of the N.Y. Philharmonic Orchestra, Lord & Taylor (A&B) created a marvelous architectural extravaganza of sweeping stairways — mezzanines — balustrades — foyers and dripping crystal chandeliers to acknowledge the occasion and to show off their collection of black and garnet velvet evening gowns. They even had their male mannequins dressed in tux to escort the ladies up and down the stairs and to the special performance. Memorabilia tied in with the illustrious history of the orchestra was displayed in the architectural setting and a giant sheet of music in the corner window helped to set the musical theme for the battery of windows.

The Black and White Ball
An Affair to Remember

Friday, January
Little America
7 p.m. until midnight
call Pat 568   583-9

Proceeds go to   symphony

D

To celebrate a charity ball for a French organization that supports hospitals, Bendel's (C) showed the mannequin in her black going-to-the-ball dress with her leg up in a cast and three men in red and gold livery — in attendance. It was such an unexpected sight that passersby had to stop — to look — to read the explanatory copy card before they walked on — still smiling.

ZCMI (D) got ready for the Black and White Ball —

"An Affair to Remember" — with this striking black and white display. The columns were checkerboarded and the floor board pattern was drawn on an angle and then the floor rose up to meet and vanish into the back wall — carrying the angled lines out of eyesight. Black panels were used to define the display space for the male and female realistic mannequins — all ready for the ball. The proceeds from the ball goes to support the Utah Symphony.

A

B

Fur is a fur-ocious, fur-raising topic today and while some still cling to their minks and yearn for sables, others prefer cloth on their backs and the skins on the animals in the wild. So whether it is frankly fur — or the fur is faux — here are some presentations that can go either way.

Lush and lavish: The fur coat in the Frohlich display (A) is as real as it comes through the over-scaled red silk roses surrounding the mannequins, are definitely fake. However, the red setting, the boiserie and the big, big vibrant red roses do make an appealing statement.

Humor does it at the Galeries Lafayette (B). The fun fur is plummy pink and displayed on a dress form on an old-fashioned roll-around cast iron base. The articulated arms that are attached to the form hold a matching bag. In a spotlight of its own is the white poodle whose chain has become snagged around the base of the form. Note the way the rear wall has been "painted" with the assorted colored lights.

Mourat-Idis (C) shows its wares while actually showing very little of its wearables. The ornate gilt frames add a sense of elegance and they are combined with photo enlargements of fur coats in use. A single fur scarf and hat are draped over one of the frames — showing the real product in dimension. It is a "sampling" display with only a single sample in sight.

Fendi (D) goes to the opera in style, and the stylized mannequins are finished off with paper sculptured pompadours made of kraft paper. The background panel is a sepia print blow-up of a renaissance print designed with frames and moldings surrounding a drawing — all executed as a grisaille trompe l'oeil piece of artwork. The lighting enriches the skins and the furs and the fantasy headdresses on the mannequins.

A: Frolich Furs, Munich, Germany
    Peter Rank Designs

B: Galeries Lafayette, E. 57th St., New York, NY

C: Mourat-Idis, Washington, DC
    Displays by PROP, John Kiser

D: Fendi, Fifth Ave., New York, NY

D

C

A

B

A: **Macy's, Herald Square, New York, NY**

B: **Barneys, Seventh Ave., New York, NY**
Simon Doonan, Sr. V.P. of Advertising/Display

C: **Macy's, Herald Square, New York, NY**

C

Halloween has become the special holiday for the young — of all ages. It is time to dress up — to go out and have fun. It is definitely the time to dress for the occasion. Since the motion picture industry always seems to have a monster "monster" picture to release in October in time for Halloween chilling; another Addams Family reunion — a new Dracula rising to suck more blood or a rewrapping of the mummy. It is easy to latch on to the Horror Flick of the Moment to create an arresting window thriller. All it takes is a little stretch to tie it in with the fashions of the season.

With all the latex and vacuum-formed horror masks available in the local scare stores, and with some bandages, red dye and some imagination, it is possible to create an amusing and be-witching window. The examples we have selected are big-budget opuses that can be scaled down to smaller "screens."

Macy's (A) display coincided with the arrival of the first Addams Family film and the mannequin is dressed up as Morticia with her long, lank black hair. She is making a guest appearance in the eerie, weird and quite forlorn garden house setting. The party being attended in the other Macy display (C) could be a nightmare come true. The ballroom is shrouded with limp, moth eaten clothes and the escorts include one Frankenstein and a pair of unraveling mummies in formal wear. The setting is flooded with bloody red light.

The Barneys display (B) bows to the Vampire legend which just won't die and it has the mannequin making a Dracula-like awakening at midnight. Imagine what can still be done with flying bats — cobwebs — sheer black curtains rustling in the unseen wind — owls — and the ever-present witches. People just love to be scared — they sometimes even pay for the privilege.

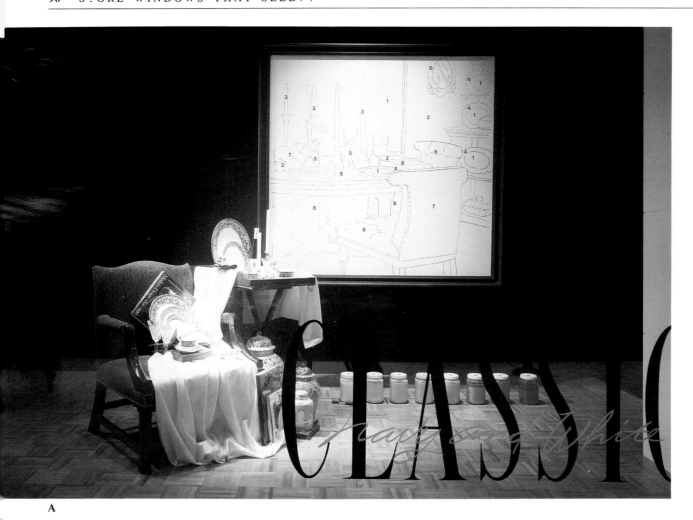

A

B

A&B: Marshall Field's, Chicago, IL
Jamie Becker, Dir. State St. Displays
Amy Meadows, Window Manager

C&D: Harvey Nichols, London, England
Mary Portas, Head of Sales Promotion and Visual
Merchandising

Home furnishings has become home fashions and what used to be dull and dreary has become smart and stylish. What used to be a display of chairs, lamps, tables and linens has become "life-style" presentations with vignettes appropriately and completely coordinated and accessorized like the latest outfit or costume. It has become "Designer" — "Fashion" — and "Art."

Marshall Field's in Chicago (A&B) plots the way with a do-it-by-the-number drawing on the back wall of the window that shows a room for living in with a personality and a theme. Up front, on the glass, as part of the store's "Classic" promotion — which also included men's and women's fashions — we are told that "Navy and White" is the team to root for. The assorted components that are outlined in the drawing appear — in full color and dimension — in a clutter arrangement in mid-window showing just how effective the mix and match can be when seen as a composition of decorative elements. In the Housewares Sale display — the designers cleverly re-interpret the logo of the promotion in wood and we get the outline suggestion of a house with a rectangle hanging in space to represent a window in the invisible structure. Balancing the construction and the message on the glass is a 3-D arrangement of assorted items to be found in the Market Place — all in white with a few dashes and a single splash of red — to recall the red lettering of the message. The expert lighting puts the products into prominence.

C

D

Harvey Nichols, the well known London fashion specialty store in Knightsbridge (C&D) combines the art of dressing with the art of furnishing with a tie-in with *Elle Decoration* magazine. The giant black and white checkerboard that fills the display space provides contrasting square of background for items standing in front of them. The unique fashion accessories — for the home — are part of "Pop Future" and they are treated as pieces of art and/or sculpture rather than useful home items.

In another window in the same *Elle Decoration* promotion headless forms are flung into the melee of rich prints and patterns and a sort of medieval setting seems to unify the assorted home fashion offerings.

A

The Marshall Field's, Chicago Home Fashions area is an important part of this classic department store and the window displays for Home Fashions often takes over the main State St. windows. They are given the same "love and care" and imaginative treatments that is usually reserved for clothes presentations. On these pages (A,C,D,E) we present some of the display department's clever approaches to Home Fashions.

The Great Outdoors (A) starts with a bleacher and a background of pennants for the home town football team — but it could just as well be for a local college or high school team. Spread out on the various levels of the built-up bleacher is a selection of home furnishings that were designed to travel and then star in the pre-game tailgate dinners or picnics that are sometimes the best part of going to the game. The presentation seems to start with the glorified hamper into which all these items will eventually fit.

Going down to the farm — and maybe a bit Southwest — brings out the "Yippie-I-Ay" display (C) where bales of hay are used as elevations and they support different but similar groupings of china. The rakes add some diagonal lines that equate movement in the composition. The same theme is also used for the display of a variety of floor and table lamps (E) and once again the designers have used the bales to make a series of viewing levels for the individual pieces pulled together in the single composition.

B

C

A,C,D,E: Marshall Field's, Chicago, IL
   Jamie Becker, Director of State St. Windows
   Amy Meadows, Window Manager

B: Jacobson's, Birmingham, MI
   Janice Cecil, Visual Merchandising Director
   Jane Chike, Assistant

D

E

In a more staid and reflective mood is "Gatherings" (D) which is a handsome, simple vignette arrangement in a gold washed space. Here the composition is classic.

From Jacobson's (B) we get this amusing picnic outing about to be totally destroyed by a wayward animal. The cloud filled blue sky — the red and white gingham cloth — and the "action" of the tilted table with everything on top of it sliding off towards disaster gains the viewer's attention and also wins a smile or two.

A

B

ZCMI in Salt Lake City is another venerable department/specialty store that has made an enviable name for itself in promoting Home Fashions and Furnishings. On these two pages we show some recent efforts and promotions.

Like the Marshall Field's "Classic" window — the color is blue and the setting is white. What makes this display so effective is the scale of the window area in relation to the few small items being presented. Instead of masking down the window — they have actually enhanced the feeling of open space with the blue lighting assisting mightily. The overall atmosphere is of a modern museum showing off unique pieces of "art." The bits of blue glass triangles floating in space lead the viewer's eye down to the striking blue glass bowl set dead center in the vast space. The rolled up blue towel beckons — but not before the eye has hopped from the silvery pot and then on to the assorted pieces of glass and steel set out on the lowest steps. A "Classic" presentation indeed.

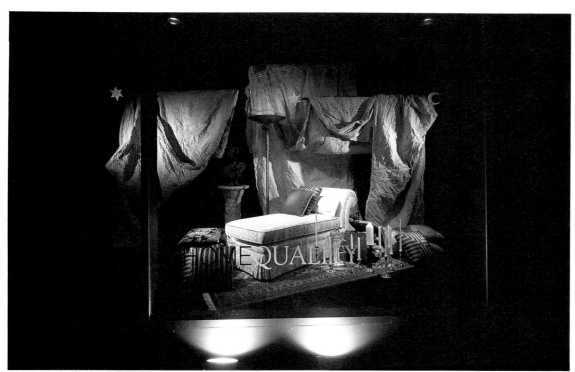

C

D

A,B,C,D: ZCMI, Salt Lake City, UT
Mike Stevens, Visual Merchandising Director
Designers: Sherri Orton (A)
Anne Cook (B)
Dennis Wardle (C&D)

To celebrate the company's 125th anniversary, they introduced a new gift wrap and (B) shows how it was done. Chrome colored housewares are combined with the shiny black bags and boxes and the torn strips of chartreuse and hot pink seamless paper used as a background. Poufs of tissue and ribbons of the same colors are stuffed in the bags and in and around the silvery products.

The theme for (C&D) was "Home: Quality" and the two vignettes are beautifully set up and lit in the all-black ambience of the windows. The startling contrast of the rough, plaster like finish of the drapery which is not "real" to the slick and smooth surfaces of the fine woods and the leather and damask upholstery makes these presentations winners. Also adding to the effectiveness is the sparkle and gleam of the polished brass accessories. Note the illuminated sun and moon finials at the ends of the rods that support the "drapery" which looks like muslin dipped in a plaster solution, squeezed out (to get all those wrinkles and texture) and then allowed to set in the pre-draped shape.

Targeting in on table settings — on China and Glass — on Silver — on all the little things — can be confusing to the shopper if not shown as "entities" — as parts of a whole, and so we have selected these examples of good solutions to the problem.

From Munich, the Tiffany & Co. display (A) is set in a small, elevated window. The back wall and the floor pads are upholstered with a warm beige fabric and, in contrast, the three pedestals are chunks of rough hewn wood. A selection of silver cascades down each pedestal and the top surface is shared by a ceramic dragon and a different design dinner plate. Off center, on the floor, are some ornate silver serving plates and bowls. Three angled cards carry the names and prices for the silver and china patterns shown above.

Bergdorf gives the same care to detail and accessorizing — the same Bergdorf "look" to the home fashions that it gives to women's and men's fashions. The seafood plates (B) swim across the wall though caught up in a fish net. The "fishy" chair complements the theme as do the applied sea grass cut out of colored paper. Sponged topiary artwork creates the outdoor setting in (C) — along with swarms of green and chartreuse sponged butterflies. The verdigris metal furniture and the colorful ceramic accessories and fabric pillows are all part of a tribute to "The Artistry, Elegance and Diversity of European Style."

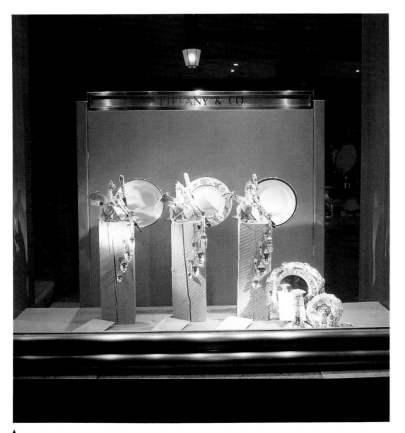

A

B

C

E

A: **Tiffany & Co., Munich, Germany**
   Peter Rank Design

B&C: **Bergdorf Goodman, Fifth Ave., New York, NY**
   Richard Currier, V.P. of Visual Presentation

D: **Fortunoff, Fifth Ave., New York, NY**
   Peter Moodie, Visual Director

E: **Liberty of London, London, England**
   Paul Muller, Director of Promotions and Visual
   Presentation

D

Lush, romantic and "European" is the lavish table set in the Fortunoff window (D) with flowers, fruit, and even a still life painting sharing the table with the china, glass and silver. In the shadowy setting, an opulent room is suggested by the twisted column, the fan window and the brocaded drapery and the decorative brass candelabra/chandelier hanging down over it all.

Peter, Peter the Pumpkin Eater couldn't have wanted more than to dine off these richly colored sunflower bedecked serving pieces in blue, orange and yellow in the Liberty of London window (E). The big, fat, shiny mache pumpkins reinforce the orange color in the ceramics presented on three levels — for better viewing — and the deep blue background turns royal blue in the flush of the warm light that is used to bring out the rich color of the merchandise.

A

B

L inens — sheets and pillowcases — towels and bath
   mats — they have come a very long way from the
   days of "White Sales" when all it took was neat
stacks of white merchandise tied up with pink ribbon bows
to sell the monotonous product. Today the color — the
patterns — the possibilities for mix and match are myriad
and here are some distinctly different looks — with more to
follow on the next pages.

From Strawbridge & Clothier (A) — another grand old
department store in the true sense — we get a simple,
Mondrian-like construction — like a skeletal armoire —
painted white and provided with a series of framed cubby-
holes in which to show off the variety of coordinated
pieces. The large central area is filled with a floral patterned quilted coverlet and surrounding it are pillow shams,
pillowcases, sheets and other items designed to go-with.
Sprays of dried flowers add another texture and a relief
from the pattern. Hanging behind; another coverlet — a
different size and a variation on the "star" in the center spot.

The Descamps company of France (B) made its name
with its mix and match approach to linens for bed and bath
— and the accessories that join in the game. In this display
the yellow terry robed mannequin is inundated by a bevy of
red, yellow and blue towels and terry products. The red,
yellow and blue palette is also carried out in the bamboo
poles, fans and ribbons that help to pull the display together.
The bed is covered with a print that combines the three
colors with white and a red sheet recalls the towels scattered
on the floor and wrapped around the mannequin's head.

F rom Ralph Lauren-Polo (C) we get this elegant and
   imaginative "cluttered" presentation. Two "antique"
   dress forms are used but only one is partially
dressed like a French provincial, 18th century shepherdess
— in Polo-designed linens and sheets. More sheets and
pillow cases are tied up and presented along with decorative pillows and throws on the wicker table on the left.
Natural grape vining entwines the linen display and like a
scene from "The Return of Martin Guerre" — the rustic
idyll is bathed in gold/amber light.

C

A: **Strawbridge & Clothier, Philadelphia, PA**
   Chris Dixon-Graff, V.M. Director

B: **Descamps, Madison Ave., New York, NY**

C: **Polo-Ralph Lauren, Madison Ave., New York, NY**

A

A&B: Castner Knott, Nashville, TN

C&D: Barneys, Seventh Ave., New York, NY
Simon Doonan, Sr. V.P. Advertising/Display

B

Castner Knott takes a "Classic" approach to their "White" promotion — and they certainly do mean "White"! Semi-realistic mannequins have been painted chalk white and we are willing to accept them as Greek or Roman gods and goddesses. And — more for selling than for the sake of modesty — they are draped with terry towels to emulate the togas of yore. More of the merchandise, neatly folded and stacked, is lined up in front of the classically draped figures. To "dress" the white paneled space, white marbleized columns are added along with fluted pedestals (all "must" items in any well furnished display warehouse) entwined with variegated ivy garlands. The lighting is low-keyed and makes the light-hearted approach seem more serious than it really is. Call it "dramatic license."

C

D

The small, open back windows that line the side of Barneys store in New York (C&D) get these opulent, fantasy treatments when it comes to home fashion accessories like throw pillows, napkins, fabrics and wallpapers. In one set-up, a wooden cart with wheels all but fills the narrow window and it is piled high with pillows, bolts of fabric and rolls of wallpaper. On the moss-covered floor, more pillows are stuffed into wood bushel baskets and apple crates — spilling over with the fruit onto the gray green floor. Panels of wallpaper are hung in a variety of height as a dimensional collage behind the cart.

The base for the arrangement in (C) is an old, semi-rusted metal flower stand which is now laden with water and mold stained clay pots and patina-ed copper watering cans. Dewy fresh, flower patterned pillows and napkins grow out of and about the earthy pots.

anie Kerley
sy of ALU

A

Far away places with strange sounding names —
romantic memories of places visited — dreams of
places to go — they all add to the drama, the
excitement and the romance of Import promotions.
Whether it is the import of the latest French fashions or the
newest from the boutiques off the Via Veneto — or fabric
woven on the moors of Scotland, or off the craggy shores
of wind-swept Ireland — the products are enhanced when
"touched" with the exotic ambience that suggests the source
or the country of origin.

A&B: Galeries Lafayette, E. 57th St., New York, NY

C: Henri Bendel, Fifth Ave., New York, NY
Barbara Putnam, Display Director

B

What says France like Paris, and what symbolizes
Paris like the sky-scratching finial that is the
Eiffel Tower; a web of criss-crossing bands of
steel that rises and rises — tier after tier until it dominates
the landscape of the City of Lights and the joie de vivre.
Galeries Lafayette (A), a noted French institution, now with
a branch in New York, explains its "lend-lease" policy
when they combine paintings of the famous French symbol
with The Lady in the Harbor who personifies the U.S. The
extravagant cape/wrap in luscious pink is by Yves St.
Laurent and the hot pink appears in the Statue of Liberty
painting and in the steamy light that floods the left side of
the display. A cool blue light balances the left hand side of
the composition. The artwork is by Stephanie Kerley. Also
at Galeries Lafayette (B) is this line-up of miniature Eiffel
Towers — in a row with the two mannequins in sepia
colored outfits in the dark, dark window. Even the models
of the tower are painted charcoal gray and the low ambient
lighting allows the emphasis lighting on the mannequins to
spill over on the floor and onto the message laid out in
black letters on the white floor.

Henri Bendel, of the French name (C) celebrates the
State of Claude Montana and his red and black leather coats
and jackets with this soaring wire framed sculpture of the
Eiffel Tower. Shiny black vinyl drapes are pulled back to
either side to frame and to reveal the red and black clad
mannequins standing on the black mica covered floor.

State of Claude Montana 94

C

A

C

B

On this page — ITALY — the land of the Classics — of the great, great Roman civilization — of art, architecture — of arches and arcades — of sculpture, opera and music. Italy is almost interchangeable with Classic (see p. 44-45).

Chanel (A), though French, salutes the Italian classics with the photo enlargement of a Venus statue overlooking a landscape of Tuscan red-tiled roofs and an elongated, fluted column that rises and disappears behind the window valance above. The walls and floor are white and a single floor-to-ceiling mirror panel adds depth — and another perspective on the garments — in the cool, airy space.

It could be Italy — but it definitely is classic for these Jaeger (B) suits shown on dress forms amid the simulated arcades and facades of Italian inspiration. The black and white checkered floor is partially covered with puddles of white marble chips and the lighting picks out the chests of the two outfits and adds some sunlight to the pediment of the unit on the left.

Pilar Rossi (C) lives up to its name with the giant Corinthian cap that serves as a seat for the realistic mannequin in the red suit. On the dark gray floor board — lost in shadows — is a pensive Venus bust — armless and beautiful. The expert lighting does add shadows to the sculptured surfaces. *Also see p. 52.*

D

A: Chanel, E. 57th St., New York, NY

B: Jaeger's, Madison Ave., New York, NY
   Display by IDEAS

C: Pilar Rossi, Madison Ave., New York, NY
   Marc Manigault, Designer

D: Liberty of London, London, England
   Paul Muller, Director of Promotions and Visual Presentation

Liberty of London (D) saluted its neighbors across the sea with an All of Ireland promotion that encom passed men's and women's wear as well as home fashions and accessories. The gray-streaked background and the landscaping up front all simulate the color and feel of Ireland and the deep green wheel and wood construction add even more texture and ambience to the setting. The costume made of Irish woolens and tweeds in red trimmed with blues and violets, stands out against the complementary green unit behind it and also from the soft gray/greens of the foliage up front.

A

B

C

A,B,C,D: Liberty of London, London, England
Paul Muller, Director of Promotions and Visual
Presentation

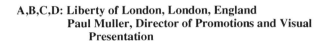

When Liberty of London goes "abroad" — it really travels first class, and they also take all of their customers along for a wondrous journey to parts exotic, romantic and sometimes only dreamed of. A&B are only two of the several displays that were used to tie in with their Indonesia promotion. Partly based on fact and more than partly on fantasy, they show Indonesia not as it necessarily is, but as we imagine and hope it will be: rich, golden, opulent, and glowingly warm. Actual pieces that have been imported for sales in the store share the display space with fantasy figures and "unreal" foliage. These dream-like, almost balletic settings are theatrically illuminated to intensify the un-real quality of the display and reassure us that Indonesia is a special place — far away — exotic — other worldly.

The Guatemala displays (C&D) are cool and remote in contrast and the Rousseau-like, dream landscape turns these lush, over-foliated green jungles into perfect complements for the strong, vibrant colors and patterns of the Guatemalan fabrics used to drape and dress the realistic mannequins. In an interior display, the jungle setting persists with the hanging strands of green stained raffia and the fabric fronds supported by almost invisible trees. On one side, black abstracts are dressed in traditional Guatemalan robes and woven fabrics — on the opposite side black abstracts and forms wear costumes and outfits that make use of these exciting colors and prints and are adapted for the contemporary woman. Raffia, straw, giant multi-colored paper flowers and woven Guatemalan belts are used to decorate the straw baskets filled with more decorative flowers and carried on the heads of some of the "native" figures. This combines display with exhibit — and furthers the theme introduced in the windows.

D

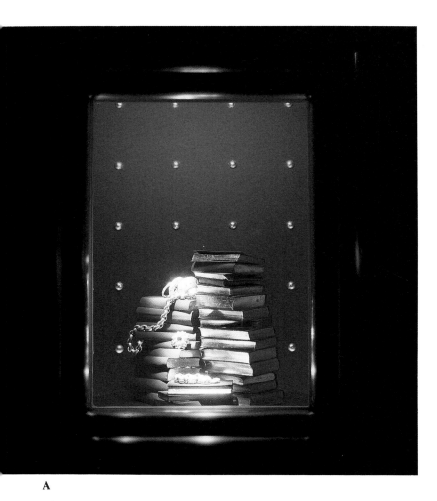

A

The Fortunoff window (C) contains a great variety of Native American silver and turquoise jewelry. The adobe construction with the rustic wooden ladder and war bonnet on top not only sets the time and place for the jewelry but it contains them in the window space which is really too large in scale for the individual products being displayed. It becomes a frame and it separates the jewelry from all the space around it. The cut-out openings, the rungs of the ladder, the protruding logs in the adobe construction — the skin-covered tom-tom and the rocks all serve as risers and elevations; partly separating and showing off some of the pieces as individual works of the silver craft. Taken all together, the setting is a treasure trove of wonderful objects — almost like what one would hope to find displayed spread out on a woven blanket on the sand in Santa Fe.

A: **Tiffany & Co., Munich, Germany**
    Peter Rank Design

B: **Ca-Da, Munich, Germany**
    Peter Rank Design

C: **Fortunoff, Fifth Ave., New York, NY**
    Peter Moodie, Display Director

B

Jewelry — whether real or costume — is small and precious and needs to be carefully showcased if it is to be seen. Ideally, pieces of jewelry are best shown off in shadow boxes; small, intimate spaces where the floor is raised up and the object to be viewed is closer to eye level. When the window is big, then the jewelry needs something larger and enveloping to take in the pieces — support them and serve to attract the shopper and bring them up to the glass where he/she can study the individual pieces — up close.

The Tiffany & Co. (A) window is the familiar style Tiffany shadow box and books are covered and stacked in uneven piles to serve as supports and elevations for the baubles being offered. The lighting is tightly controlled; it strikes just the few pieces of jewelry while the background panel appears rich and deeper due to the dark blue light that illuminates the rear wall.

Ca-Da (B), another jewelry store in Munich, also features a deep ultramarine ambience and a pair of wire bird cages, a disk covered with silver foil, some miniature step ladders and small "animated" artist's mannequins finished in charcoal inhabit the space. The floor is semi-covered with jet diamond dust and the very few pieces of jewelry are accented by sharp beams of clear light.

C

A

B

Propping jewelry can be fun. Sometimes the change of scale — or texture or just the very contrast of the subject matter can effectively set off the jewelry being presented.

At Vicenza Oro (A) a simulated bird's nest, some twigs and a few feathers are used to show off the gold bracelets — fine and delicately crafted — against the rough, uneven surface of the woven nest. A few colorful feathers scattered about on the dark floor underscore and accentuate some other pieces of gold.

Make your move! It is croquet time at Lampert's (B) where the designer has taken the lawn game and moved the mallets and balls into the darkened space where the jewelry is displayed on black grid panels. Other games could also work.

With Halloween on the way, Bogart (C) filled its clean, contemporary window with rustic twig brooms that any witch could be proud to call her own. The scale of the broom contrasts sharply with the small precious pieces displayed on the series of white lucite risers and shelves.

The master of the unique prop — for jewelry display — must be Gene Moore of Tiffany & Co. N.Y., (D,E,F) and his props can include anything from fine arts, sculpture, fabulous goods, specially crafted miniatures dressed in opulent costumes to completely unexpected dimensional collage pieces like that shown in (E). In each instance, Gene Moore's venue is a small raised shadow box with a background lit from below and behind. A few well-aimed mini-spots will then pick out the one-of-a-kind piece of jewelry that is often found in the foreground — closest to the glass and the viewer.

C

A: Vicenza Oro, Lima, Peru
Karina Barhumi, Designer

B: Lester Lampert, Chicago, IL
Bruce Bliss, Designer
Photo: Matthew Alsculer

C: Bogart Jewelry, Sloane St., London, England

D,E,F: Tiffany & Co., New York, NY
Gene Moore, Display Director

D

E

F

A

C

B

eather: more than motorbikes and "The Wild One"
— more than gangs roaring about — more than
"Grease" and the '50s and '60s — more style and
stylish than ever.

Nothing can stop the clock at Henri Bendel (A) where it
is ticking for the black leather coats, hats and pants with
just a touch of an animal print to break up the monochro-
matic scheme. The black and white upholstered chairs not
only act as seats, they become props and add some diagonal
line action to the scene.

Barneys (B) combines black and red leather worn by
white semi-abstracts with large mounted photo blow-ups of
noted personalities — in black and white. The caption on
the floor reads "Acting Heads" since the subjects are actors
and way up front, near the glass, is a line of quotation that
sort of relates the foreground to the background. For
another Black and Red Leather display see p. 102-103.

Calvin Klein's merchandise at Macy's (C) is presented
graphically, too. The "old gang of mine" group picture in
the dark wood frame behind the draper with the black
leather jacket is right out of a Klein magazine ad — and it
is as recognizable as the name Calvin Klein — or Marky
Mark. A neutral sisal mat covers the floor — and the whole
neutral setting is signature Klein.

D

A: Henri Bendel, Fifth Ave., New York, NY
   Barbara Putnam, Display Director

B: Barneys, Seventh Ave., New York, NY
   Simon Doonan, Sr. V.P. Advertising/Display

C: Macy's, Herald Square, New York, NY

D: Place Desjardins, Montreal, Quebec
   Decors Yves Guilbeault, Inc.
   Photo: Andre Doyon

In a more dramatic manner, Place Desjardins (D) showed off the highly styled black leather jacket in a torrid window illuminated with more red light. The boldly, over-scaled painting of a man in a black leather jacket with body hugging leather trousers made a dynamic impact on the shopper in the street and contrasted, in scale, most effectively with the realistic mannequin in the hot environment. The grid shadow cast on the rear wall added some pattern to the otherwise under-decorated surfaces.

A

It's another blowout (C) and this time the space is filled with assorted colored lights dangling from the ceiling — wrapped around the big white cubes that act as an architectural setting/divider in the open back window — and strewn across the floor trailing in and out amidst the mannequins in their harlequin-inspired outfits. Punchinello-style, black comical hats decorated with fluffy white balls — with shoes to match — turn this display into a carnival and the most sophisticated little circus in town.

**A,B,C: North Beach Leather, Madison Ave., New York, NY
Frank Lehman, Display Director**

B

There's lots more color — style and fashion in leather than black and red! At North Beach Leather on Madison Ave. it always seems to be party time as the bright, festive colors are boldly presented with flair and imagination on both male and female mannequins.

Leather for New Year's Eve — and gala occasions? Why not? Chains of mirror pieces dangle, twist and turn in the open backed space adding piercing highlights to the already sparkling sequined and jewel trimmed outfits. The jester caps finished with glass ornaments add to the party feeling as does the giant, jewel encrusted ball that sits on the white floor which is accented with black squares of tile.

It is all in the geometric equation. (B) Mondrian designs of assorted rectangles and right angled shapes of assorted colors are stitched together in the soft supple leathers to affect these jackets and coats worn with equally bright shirts and pants. Swirls and squiggles of fat plastic tubing float in space contrasting with the sharp straight lines of the outfits and a few dollar signs are stuck in just to make sure you were really looking.

C

A

B

A,B,C: North Beach Leather, Boston, MA
Kristin Lauer, Blue Potato, Designer

D: Sims Ltd., Minneapolis, MN
Mike Vye, Display Director

Only a few hundred miles away — a completely different approach to similar merchandise — in a different and difficult window and executed by another creative designer working on a tight budget that is stretched by a wild imagination.

Taking the name of the game as her inspiration, the designer of North Beach Leather's Boston store (A) has bodies writhing, wiggling and wriggling through the space that is filled with blow-ups of the Twister cards and spinners. The bright primary colors of the cards are the same as those of the merchandise and the viewer catches here a leg — there an arm — a back view — a chest — and occasionally, an almost full figure (far left).

What could be more remote than stuffed fish floating in a gray mottled space divided by copper rain drain pipes. The male figures wear leather coats with aviator helmets — with goggles — and act almost as though they were in a Martin Cruz Smith Russian spy novel. It is the very far fetched and the strange juxtapositioning that works for the sophisticated audience who shops in this store.

D

C

Most yuppies in their 30s and 40s — and maybe even older — remember Marlo Thomas as "That Girl" on TV — Marlo with her flipped-up, long black hair. These yellow leather dresses — part of the renaissance of the '70s look — and a little bit of Courreges thrown in — appear on the Marlo Thomas look-alike mannequins and the window space is filled with graphic designs that restate over and over again — That Girl. The

TV monitor, up front plays snips of the vintage TV series.

In Minneapolis, at Sims Ltd. (D), the leather jacket gets a kind of casual, out-of-doors setting — just right for the more traditional, upscaled customer who shops there. A back wall fence made of weathered planks has a "window" applied to it to suggest a country cabin. The bare bush up front sets the season as do the fir trees and the snow underfoot. *Also see p. 66, p. 71.*

A

B

Lingerie means soft and silky underthings — the most personal of garments — the most feminine; robes and nightgowns — chemises, bras and panties. Lingerie calls for lush, sensuous boudoir settings — or does it? Mother's Day is a great time for showing off one's lingerie so do look it up on p. 150-155 — for some more approaches to this under-statement.

Bergdorf (A) presents a woman's world — a world of her own. Though her lingerie is soft and feminine, she is actually building up her mind and acumen. The wicker couch is strewn with books and more books are piled up on the floor in front of the mannequin. On the front glass is sketched a window frame with a window shade pulled up so that the "peeping Toms" who are looking in are surprised to see that this is no "Billie Dawn" — all body and no brains — but the woman of the '90s who likes to pamper herself with gentle underthings while she toughens up to meet the competition out there.

In a more relaxed mood (B) — these coordinated pieces of lingerie are shown in a simple composition with the swing supported by cerise and yellow ribbons and bows sort of tying the three realistic figures together in an asymmetrical composition.

D

A&B: **Bergdorf Goodman, Fifth Ave., New York, NY**
Richard Currier, V.P. of Visual Presentation

C&D: **Saks Fifth Avenue, New York, NY**
William Viets, V.P. of Visual Merchandising

C

Saks Fifth Ave. (C) has a robe that will travel and the dress form fitted with an upholstered egg head wears the creamy white robe. The satchels and bags fill in the idea of traveling and the soft pliable fabrics of the draped garments are all made of imported woolens.

(D) You know the story of The Princess and The Pea? Well, there are a lot more peas and pods tucked in under these mattress but the red haired princess may still be awake just because she likes to look at her fairy-tale night gown. The chandelier, overhead says "palace" and the pea pods in the spotlight on the floor say that a pea must be there — somewhere. It is the princess in the rosy light that really tells this "happily ever after" lingerie story.

We introduced the Mall displays in our entry under Denim (see p. 62-63). The idea is to show off a wide variety of retail products — fashion, accessories — even home furnishings — from a wide selection of retailers in the mall but all unified into a single strong story. For such a display to succeed in a mall setting it must make a dynamic statement either by its size — by its color or by repetition of the theme. The display must be able to compete with the movement, the lights, the color, the signage and the hundreds of people moving all around the mall and the display setting.

The Owings Mills displays (A&B) keyed in with Fall and the return to school and college. Rather than getting specific, the designers used the giant build-ups of three dimensional shapes in the strong, basic colors which could be seen from almost anyplace in the mall and from any level. These heroic scaled constructions acted as beacons — the also called out to the shoppers and showed them the way. As for the merchandise; the accent was on plaids and solids — all sorts and combinations of bright colors with black and white. The shapes of the towers also served as colorful backdrops for the garments.

A&B: Owings Mills Town Center, Owings Mills, MD
Gregory Baranoski, Visual Merchandising Director
Kay Muse, Creative Director

C, D & E: White Marsh Mall, Baltimore, MD
Jeri Lugo, Creative Visual Director
and the V.M. Team

B

A

White Marsh Mall — just the other side of Balti more celebrated their 10th anniversary and they invited the retailers to submit outfits that could be incorporated into the anniversary theme and the color scheme selected for the occasion. The palette consisted of sharp and striking purple, cerise, orange, and a vibrant blue/green. Some pieces of furniture were used to create the groupings for the mannequins and the puffy pillows reiterated the stinging, clashing colors on the graphic scheme. Floppy hats and wide swaths of scarves were created by the display team and embellished with the White Marsh name. The views presented on the right show some of the ledges in the mall and how they were arranged. Note the individual credit cards at the feet of the mannequins giving the name of the retailer who provided the garment worn by the mannequin.

C

D

E

A

**A,B,C,D: Willowbrook Mall, Wayne, NJ
Jeri Lugo and Glenn Sokoli, Designers**

B

The designers of the displays in the Willowbrook Mall have gone to all heights — figuratively — and literally — to create effective presentations in their two level mall. A&B are examples of an all American salute — appropriate for the Fourth of July — Memorial Day — or even a President's Birthday sale even in February. Obviously, the color scheme was simply red, white and blue and almost all the fashion retailers could get in on that theme — with or without stars and stripes. A bold move and a successful one was to use the giant American flag — almost two stories tall — used as the background with a set-up on either side of it. Once again, it was hard not to see the flag from any vantage point in the mall. Understanding that people see these displays from both the first and second levels of the mall, the designers used tall step ladders to bring some of the dressed mannequins up closer to those on the second tier of shops. Wherever possible, sneakers or tennis shoes were used in white, red or blue and special red baseball caps trimmed with stars and stripes were also used to unify the assorted outfits.

C

To celebrate the Olympic Games — the colors yellow, red, green, black, and blue were used and flags of all the United Nations became the major decorative props. A giant U.S.A., white silk Olympic banner dominated the main display platform and in keeping with the five colors used in the interlocking circles, five mannequins — one in each color — were lined up and long swags of silken streamers flew from the mannequins up to the mall ceiling. The special suits were trimmed with miniature banners, wide white sashes and special hats that combined the ring color with white. Hundreds of flags were plugged into the amoeba-shaped playform. The same colors and theme appeared in the center s graphic during this promotion.

D

A&B: **Willowbrook Mall, Wayne, NJ**
          Jeri Lugo and Glenn Sokoli, Designers

C&D: **White Marsh Mall, MD**
          Jeri Lugo, Visual Merchandising Creative Director

ometimes a single color — or no color — can make a powerful effect in a mall space overwhelmed with, and by, color. In this technicolored, polychromatic world we live in — which is even more concentrated in a mall — the greatest impact is to take all color away as they did in Willowbrook (A&B) when they did their all-white extravaganza. Rather than depend upon props or gimmicks — this display was done with yards and yards of semi-sheer white fabric which was hung as panels from the mall ceiling — used as banners — shirred around a base or draped over chairs and couches. To further reinforce the illusion all the mannequins were fitted with white wigs and wore the same pearl and donut drop clip earrings. The hats, bows and snoods were created by the designers and staff to finish off the outfits. When to use white? How about right after Christmas as a relief from all that red, green, and gold, or as a January or June "bridal" promotion.

Pretty and pink — they go together and White Marsh Mall (C&D) greeted Spring with a pink promotion that extended from the palest pastel pink up to the hottest and most sensuous of lipstick pinks and fuchsia. To add to the soft, gentle ambience there were lots of frothy tulle used and flower pots were wrapped with pink satin and giant pink rosebuds sprouted off the green topiary trees set in the pots. In the two views we have selected we see one of the pastel stages and another with the more vivid pink outfits.

A

B

C

D

A

B

For a summer promotion at Willowbrook Mall (A&B) white wicker furniture, white urns and flower pots overflowing with greenery and green grass carpeting was all it took to unify the strong, fresh summery outfits into a single theme. More often than not, the mall designer must stage the action as theater in the round. Unlike a window that is oriented to the traffic, the mall stage is the ultimate island display platform which can be, and is, viewed by people coming from all directions and there can't be a back or a front — but there has to be a continuous flow. Here we show the same ledge as seen from one side and then from the other to prove the point. Note how the colors are balanced and coordinated and the kids are realistically clustered together just as the women mannequins are "related" on the couch.

C

D

A&B: Willowbrook Mall, Wayne, NJ
Jeri Lugo/Glenn Sokoli, Designers

C&D: Tysons Corner, McLean, VA
Prop: John Kiser

Tysons Corner (C&D) puts on a home furnishing spectacular and for the occasion built a few industrial-type scaffolds upon which they could show couches, chairs and even more vignettes. The elevated presentations, here, also, provided more interest for the persons on the second level of the mall. The main stages — raised up about three feet from the floor carried the major presentations which combined pieces of furniture with specially selected home fashion accessories to create interesting and theatrical settings that took full advantage of the height offered by the mall location.

Gabbana on 6

A

B

MAN is a many splendored thing! He is an animal of many moods and many temperaments — and MAN has only recently discovered the world of Fashion; that he has options — choices — a selection to choose from — and ways to dress the man he is or wants to be. On the following pages we will show different approaches to dressing the man who will sometimes strut like a peacock in bright colors and other times, like an ostrich, hide in the sands of neutrality.

Men's clothing — like women's — can be shown on mannequins — on forms — on drapers or hangers. The mannequins are more often than not semi-realistic though realistic mannequins are available. The semi-realistic one will have features and hair sculpted in but will be devoid of make-up; it is usually finished in a single color. The mannequins in the Saks display (C) and the ones in Rori (D) are examples of the realistic type while the Barneys (B) and Saks (A) feature classic examples of the semi-realistic or stylized male mannequin; no make-up — no hair — and finished in white.

C

A: **Saks Fifth Ave., New York, NY**
    Matt Reed, Director of Men's Windows

B: **Barneys, Seventh Ave., New York, NY**
    Simon Doonan, Sr. Vice President Advertising/Display

C: **Saks Fifth Ave., New York, NY**
    Matt Reed, Director of Men's Windows

D: **Rori, Caracas, Venezuela**
    Carlos Brarezonsi, Display Director

D

Propping the Man's display is really no different from propping a woman's display. It takes imagination and it takes simple and familiar pieces used in unusual ways — or unique items handled in the most mundane manner. The muslin wrapped bundles bound with black silk ribbons in Saks Fifth Ave. (A) could be anything — but they do add a curious interest and add intrigue to the dramatic black and white Dolce y Gobbana outfit — with beret — worn by the mannequin in the eerie light of the window. However, the very unusual painted piece on the floor in (C) just sits there — with a special light on it — and it does replay the golden color of the man's suit — adding interest and detracting nothing.

Barneys (B) does things with pizzazz and the Frank Geary museum-quality bentwood lounge chair shares the window with the formally dressed mannequin. Behind — everything seems to have come apart; the assorted, unassembled pieces of bentwood are just piled up in back. A unique piece of sculpture on a plywood panel balances the "mess."

In an international gesture of good-will the Rori display (D) features a large cast of realistic male mannequins backed up with a colorful array of flags of many friendly nations. It also implies that many of the Rori fashions are imported from fashion centers and designers from around the world.

en's fashion stores, like women's stores, should create visual images that appeal to their targeted customers. Here we show several windows that appeared in Sims, Ltd. in downtown Minneapolis: a sophisticated, up-scale men's specialty shop that carries top-line clothes that are "safe" but far from "stuffy."

In a striking set of windows the designer did a series of graphic images that tied in with local, well-known, restaurants. The display-person used forms — carefully rigged, draped and shaped — and then he suspended them against backgrounds alive with graphic and even actual table settings — seen from a new perspective. In window (B) a tribute was paid to The Pickled Parrot and their slogan — "The Heat Is On." They specialize in Caribbean foods. The new French Cafe (C) in the Warehouse district is now part of the Minneapolis "gallery scene" and its bar is called "The Art Bar." This is the smart, stylish scene and the clothes reflect that sense of life-style dressing.

A

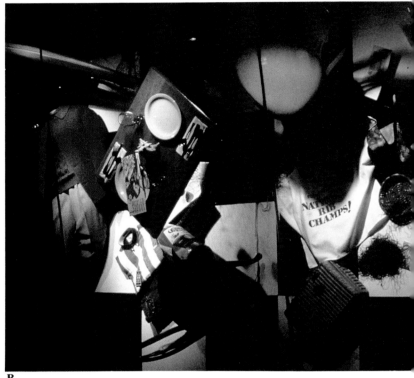

B

C

D

The flavor and excitement of the Southwest is captured in Tejas (D) and to fully create the spirit of the place the designer turned a completely-set table on end. Here the clothes are casual and colorful. One of *Esquire*'s "top ten single's bars" is located in Minneapolis and to affect the Yukon flavor of The Loon Cafe, the designer added Alaskan-type artifacts and memorabilia — as well as the rugged, out-of-door clothes one would expect to wear — up there. For each set-up the clothes that were selected carried out the life-style — the attitude — or kind of attire right for the restaurant portrayed in a dramatic and yet amusing manner.

As a spring window (A), the designer created a dimensional pattern of torn blobs of white seamless paper which were semi-applied to the black, back wall. The dressed, suspended forms were dressed in black and white. A white cylinder projects forward from the rear wall to bring a "seated" form closer to the front glass.

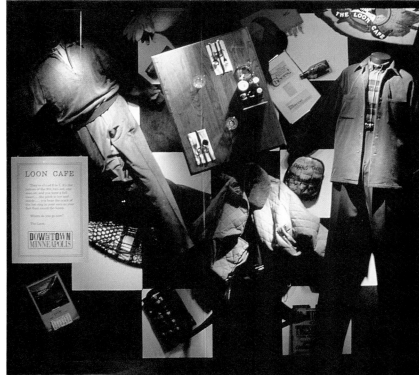

E

A,B,C,D,E: Sims Ltd., Minneapolis, MN
Mike Vye, Display Director

This noted designer's store, on Fifth Ave., has developed a signature style in their displays that is as much a trademark as the logo on the window. In a rather limited space, with a window that reaches almost down to the ground, and a movable back wall — the merchandise is always flawlessly and beautifully presented on suit forms. Mannequins are never used but they are simulated with the hip length forms plus some expert draping and shaping. In conjunction with the form or forms almost always a piece of graphics or a photo enlargement is used. What makes the dressing of the forms so effective is the suggested animation and dimension that gets into each display — the way the drapability or "hand" of the fabric is shown — the softness, the texture and the feel of the fabric enhanced by the soft, dramatic lighting — AND — the totally professional presentation of the garments.

A: Three forms in echelon are supported by black metal stands. Note the easy stance — the hands in the pockets — the slight pouf of the ties — and the Zegna catalogues tucked under the imaginary arms.

B: The same easy-going, relaxed feeling of the dressed form — all in off-white with a blue sweater tied around the waist. The blue and white photo blow-up complements the outfit and balances it in the simple, asymmetric display.

C: Behind, a gauzy-gray photo of a woman eyeing the forms in the equally soft gray Zegna suit. Across the front glass are angular strips of frosted acetate that add to the illusionary quality of the photo in the rear — and makes the shopper get closer to see the suit sandwiched between.

A

B

C

Cashmere

D

A,B,C,D: Ermenegildo Zegna, Fifth Ave., New York, NY

D The soft feel of Cashmere. The jacket in the photo is the jacket shown on the form and one can almost feel the sensuous softness of the gold scarf wrapped around the form's neck plate. Here one can appreciate the artistry of the draping — and the expert lighting that reinforces the message.

A

The lowly, misused, abused and often discarded clothes hanger — of wire but preferably wood — takes on stature and provides "shoulders" for these menswear displays. The examples on these pages show what and how garments — complete outfits fully accessorized — can be presented in real displays that attract and intrigue. Though they don't really show how things fit and they are not as flattering to the garments as forms or figures would be, they do provide a sense of style — of panache — and a good idea as to how the various parts will come together. The hanger may be suspended invisibly from above but it is more usual to see it hooked off a wall or held up by a wood or metal stand which is called a draper. A draper combines a hanger and sometimes a slack bar and it is self standing. As the viewer will note there is no attempt at padding or tissue poufing to simulate a "body"; the garments either hung square or draped to droop — but with a personality of its own.

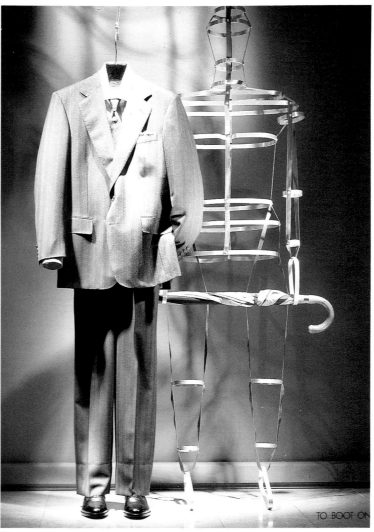

B

C

A&B: **Bergdorf, Store for Men, Fifth Ave., New York, NY**
George Shimko, Display Director

C: **Saks Fifth Ave., New York, NY**
William Viets, Vice President of Visual Merchandising
Matt Reed, Men's Window Manager

D: **Harvey Nichols, London, England**
Mary Portas, Head of Sales Promotion and Visual
Merchandising

D

In Bergdorf's Store for Men (A) an outfit is hung askew in the black ambience of the window. An interesting and amusing elephant head — hung off the wall — supports the sagging suit. In a separate spotlight on the floor is a pile of peanuts. The (B) window combines a wire frame and metal strap sculpture of a figure with a suit completely accessorized and hung off a hanger which is supported from above. A fashionable umbrella is carried by the metal sculpture and other accessories could have been draped over that very drapable figure.

Saks Fifth Ave. (C) gets scholarly and provides a stack of leather bound books to accompany the educated hanger on a draper. Atop the tomes — a cluster of grapes and a pocket handkerchief casually draped in the deep red/amber light of the window.

Harvey Nichols display (D) shows off some Joseph Abboud outfits on drapers. The setting is fall; textures abounds. The background is checkerboarded with squares of natural plywood — knot holes and all — played plyed grain against grain. The floor and the bases of the drapers are covered with coarse sawdust and sprouting from the open necks of the outfits are neutral, natural dried foliage.

C

B

A

The master of illusion — of make-believe people filling make-believe spaces and doing impossible things on Madison Ave. is Thomas Beebe and his fellow magicians who with each trim cast an enchantment over the smart shoppers who pass their windows. Often the run of windows will be a clever and often audacious take-off on a theme with each window — whether featuring invisible men or women — will tell another part of the "story." The forms which are used almost exclusively will wear hats or head-dresses over non-existent heads, carry or "support" props with armless sleeves and handless gloves or seem to move about full of imagination on imagined legs. It is all done with lighting — and brilliant technique. The black, black window spaces are brilliantly pin-pricked with sharp beams of light that accentuate the positive — the things that are there — and move past the things that aren't. Props galore are used and they are often everyday, easy-to-find or borrow things that actually gain in stature as they appear as the supporting cast to the imaginary stars.

(B) is an example of a theme that can and does delight the Madison Ave. shopper as he/she goes from window to window relishing not only the clothes presented but the clever props that carry forth the theme. Using familiar expressions or axioms — cliche expressions — the designers created this setting for "Don't Let The Cat Out of the

A,B,C,D: Paul Stuart, Madison Ave., New York, NY
Thomas Beebe, Creative Director
Jerry Fredella and Michael Verbert, Visual Directors

D

Bag." The headless form wears a pile-up of hats which is explained by the book it is reading "The Cat in the Hat" and the other hand holds the burlap bag with the cat that shouldn't be allowed to escape. Note the white mouse on the figure's shoulder safe in the knowledge that the cat is in captivity.

(C) is done with draping — and no form at all. A pair of picture frames are used in the all-black setting. The larger,

bandaged frame shows off the hat, coat, scarf and matching umbrella while more umbrellas plus shoes appear contained within the lower frame.

(D) allows you to enjoy the perfection of the illusion; the complete, smart and sophisticated man-about-town accented with an incongruous but delicious candied apple on a stick. It is part of a Big Apple salute and silhouettes of apples appear on the front glass.

A

A: **Saks Fifth Ave., New York, NY**
   William Viets, Vice President of Visual Merchandising
   Matt Reed, Menswear Window Manager

B: **Paul Stuart, Madison Ave., New York, NY**
   Thomas Beebe, Creative Director

C: **Bergdorf, Store for Men, Fifth Ave., New York, NY**
   Richard Currier, Vice President of Visual Presentation
   George Shimko, Director of Mens Store Windows

D: **H.A.&E. Smith, Hamilton, Bermuda**
   Wm. H. Collieson, Display Director

B

Sweaters and such sporty items for men. The Saks Fifth Ave. window (A) shows off Joseph Abboud sweaters and outerwear jackets on hangers hung off drapers with the entire layered outfit arranged off the single hanger. A pair of grids fashioned from 1x4 raw lumber hang tilted over the forms with light accentuating the pattern of the grids and the neutral fall coloration. Balancing the act is a giant sphere of the world wrapped with bands that carry the message — "Just One World."

As a follow-up window to the Paul Stuart display described on p. 136 is this one (B) which tells us the "Watch Before You Leap." The two imagined figures in colorful and patterned sweaters are surrounded by a plague of oversized green frogs that overwhelm the space. By looking closely around the missing heads you can see some of the strip that were pulled to pull off this illusion.

D

C

An outdoors setting for fall is suggested in the Bergdorf window (C) where the mottled, Pompeiian red background is accented with paint stained and weathered wooden louvers and a vase filled with dried sunflowers. The very traditional draper has a shirt form on top layered with a sport shirt and cardigan sweater while the slack bracket that extends off the supporting rod carries a pair of folded trousers. On the floor — a pair of shoes and a small identifying sign. The single angled louver breaks up the straight and vertical line arrangement of the composition — relaxing it to complement the casual styled merchandise.

When composition is all and the merchandise is treated as the lines and masses in that composition; we turn to the H.A.&E. Smith display (D). The colors and patterns are carefully coordinated and the lighting doesn't so much emphasize a single piece as it adds shadows and thus depth and dimension to this 3-D arrangement of men's casual wear.

A

B

Men's coats are shown as fashionable toppers to business suits in these displays. Saks Fifth Ave. (A) has three Flemish Renaissance style chairs lined up separating the two dressed suitforms with the topcoats casually pulled back to reveal the suits and coordinates beneath. Swinging across the window, in a change of style and attitude but gaining attention, is a heavy pulley and a rough rope slide that carries and holds a single hat over the central chair. The incongruous introduction of the industrial with the sophisticated makes this otherwise formal and symmetrical presentation relax and ease up.

In a more "classic" setting of thin columns lined up behind the floor-to-ceiling, high-tech friction pole that supports the dressed form is Aquascutum's coat and suit display (B). A pile of white marble chips breaks up the formality of the black and white checkered tile floor and an open black umbrella all but hides a second form in another raincoat.

D

A series of books on Modern Art and artists is lined up against the front window at Barneys (C). The three part screen behind the draped hanger/draper is also decorated with a group of contemporary paintings. Here, too, the entire costume rests on and falls from the hanger and the sharp, clear light plays up the feel of the fabric and the relaxed drapability of the garments.

Another Zegna display (D) (see p. 132-133) which makes effective use of a photo blow-up. While the three-some up front stride towards the front glass and casually reveal the scarves and suits as well as the coats, the three musketeers that recede into the background show off the backs of similar garments — and also add a feeling of depth to the display. It is also an excellent example of color highlighting no color: the splash of the red scarf in dead center makes a vivid statement in the mostly neutral setting.

C

A: Saks Fifth Ave., New York, NY
William Viets, Vice President of Visual Merchandising
Matt Reed, Menswear Display Manager

B: Aquascutum, Fifth Ave., New York, NY
Design by IDEAS

C: Barneys, Seventh Ave., New York, NY
Simon Doonan, Senior Vice President Advertising/Display

D: Zegna, Fifth Ave., New York, NY

A

C

ome of the many approaches one can take with Men's Formal Wear are shown here along with Barneys (B) on p. 128. The approach can be utterly masculine and semi-serious as shown in Lazoff's (A) where both formal wear and semi-formal outfits are shown in a vignette of furniture and framed pictures. The gold drape starts on top — next to the mirrored panel on the left that replays the whole scene — and it wends its way between the elevated forms and down to the floor where it introduces the champagne bottles and the spilled ice cubes that add the celebratory note to the display. A shiny black dog and an equally shiny pair of black shoes rest on the floor and the flowing gold drapery is enriched with the Lazoff logo.

B

he silver leafed back wall in Marshall Field's window (B) is patterned with an orderly arrangement of white silk carnation boutonnieres. In the foreground — minus flower — is a black semi-abstract mannequin dressed in a tux with arms bent and legs spread; an active pose for a formal outfit that will appeal to the younger men who think of formal wear as stuffy and confining.

Once again — a fun-filled and imaginative display from Paul Stuart (C) where the old year and the new year meet in a star spattered window. The floating top hats carry the years going and coming and the staff and the long white beard represent the one that was while the trumpet and the sand and brass hour glass heralds the one that is coming.

A: Lazoff, Puerto Rico
   Frank Caballero, Display Director

B: **Marshall Field's, Chicago, IL**
   Jamie Becker, State St. Window Director
   Amy Meadows, Window Manager

C: **Paul Stuart, Madison Ave., New York, NY**
   Thomas Beebe, Creative Director

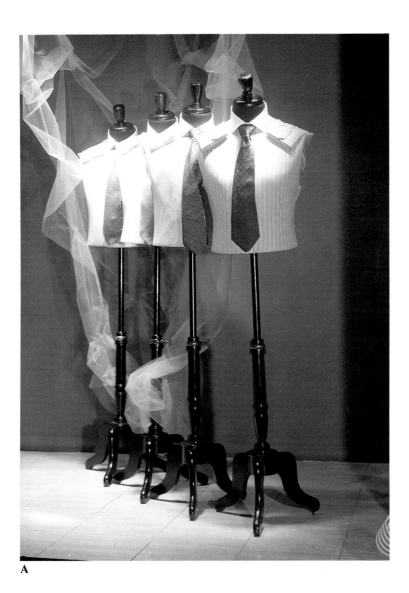

A

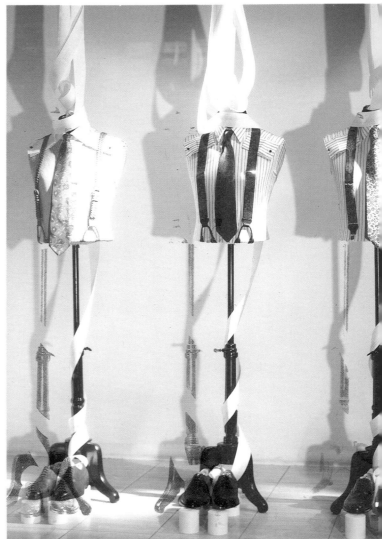

**A,B,C: Bergdorf Goodman, Fifth Ave., New York, NY
Richard Currier, Vice President of Visual Presentation**

**D: Jordan Marsh, Boston, MA
Cindy Thrana, Boston Visual Merchandising Director**

B

ashion Accessories for Men: they separate the navy from all the other navies — they make the grays seem new and "this year's" and they make the neutral backgrounds for colorful happenings. Shirts are shown with ties — sometimes with sweaters — usually with suits, slacks and sports jackets but here are shirts — mostly on their own though sometimes supported by ties and suspenders.

Bergdorf makes use of the traditional wood bases and black poles to show off their shirts and ties carefully folded and pleated on shirt forms. Streams of gauzy net (A) break up the regimental correctness of the four forms set back, echelon style, one behind the other.

D

Rolls of adding machine tape roll down from the ceiling (B) over the three suspender trimmed shirt forms — spiraling around the supporting rods and bases to end up — with some additional rolls on the floor acting as elevations for the shoes. The shirts are omitted in (C) and the decorative black forms are appliqued with shirts, ties, handkerchiefs and red tomato pin cushions used singly (on the forms) or in clusters as "heads" atop the forms. Additional folded shirts are arranged off the slack rod attachments and the yellow tapemeasures are applied onto the front glass as frames; providing convenient blocks of merchandise for individual viewing. As stated in our Couture spread, these elements — the pin cushions and the tapemeasures — add a "custom tailoring" quality to the display by their presence.

In a more relaxed and colorful presentation, Jordan Marsh (D) spreads out its wares across the whole long window and uses a variety of colored and patterned pedestals — of assorted heights — to carry out the Classic theme which is fully envisioned in the classic pediment arch on the right. Since the shirts are all colored, squares of color are laid on the white floor to further emphasize the promotion. The rear wall is tinted a gentle, neutral mauve color that complements the assembled shirts.

(Also see Father's Day.)

C

A

A: Burberry's, E. 57th St., New York, NY
   Michael Stewart, Display Director

B: Bergdorf, Store for Men, Fifth Ave., New York, NY
   George Shimko, Display Director

C: Barneys, Seventh Ave., New York, NY
   Simon Doonan, Senior Vice President, Advertising/Display

D: Saks Fifth Ave., New York, NY
   William Viets, Vice President of Visual Merchandising
   Matt Reed, Menswear Window Manager

E: Sola for Men, Cambridge, CA
   Kristin Lauer, Blue Potato, Boston

B

Ties are the truly distinctive fashion accessories for men; they are the personal statements — the bright and unexpected splash of color — the dash of excitement that enlivens a staid and stolid suit. Like the plumes that decorated men's hats in days long gone — this is the panache that a man can flaunt — wear with style — declare his individuality.

A statue of an art deco-ish archer, minus his bow and arrow, stars in the Burberry dimly lit space (A). His strong outstretched arm makes an ideal resting place — at eye level — for the mass display of ties. A shirt is casually tossed on top of the oddly-shaped but beautifully-polished log that serves as a base for the sculpture in the window.

The mass display in Bergdorf's window (B) is centered around a suit form wearing just a few furled ties. Contained within a classic pediment frame of marble are several rows of ties — one overlapping the other — and a warm light spills down from overhead in the center of the window. An ornate gilt frame (wood, gesso or vacuum formed) could also work.

PHY BY HENNY GARFUNKEL

C

E

D

Barneys does it with a twist; the white covered shirt forms stand on natural wood bases and a miniature form is set between them. Unrelated to the ties are the photographs pinned onto the back wall. The nice twist is the way the ties are neatly and meticulously "flung" around the neck plates of the forms; the tie fronts hang down in an orderly manner in the front and the tails are lost behind.

Saks (D) does its combination of furled and straight in a variation of the Bergdorf set up. The excitement of the shirts, ties, scarves, and shoes that crawl over the suit form is balanced by the somewhat serene rear wall with the ties not in an absolutely straight line — but dipping and rising as it goes.

For its trendy customers, Sola for Men in Cambridge (E) used a convenient — if not new — aluminum step ladder to provide elevations for their tie presentation. A black vinyl swath drips from step to step making a background for the ties while other ties hang in the darkness to the right of the ladder.

In all of these displays, the stores are promoting the wide range of colors, patterns and styles of ties they carry — not a particular design or designer. (Also see Father's Day.)

A

B

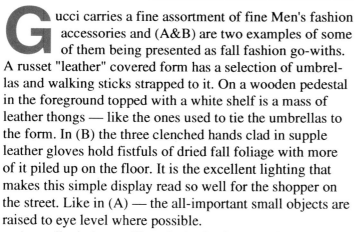

Gucci carries a fine assortment of fine Men's fashion accessories and (A&B) are two examples of some of them being presented as fall fashion go-withs. A russet "leather" covered form has a selection of umbrellas and walking sticks strapped to it. On a wooden pedestal in the foreground topped with a white shelf is a mass of leather thongs — like the ones used to tie the umbrellas to the form. In (B) the three clenched hands clad in supple leather gloves hold fistfuls of dried fall foliage with more of it piled up on the floor. It is the excellent lighting that makes this simple display read so well for the shopper on the street. Like in (A) — the all-important small objects are raised to eye level where possible.

A small window at Sims, Ltd. (C) showed off a special pair of sandals walking on what-could-be-softer-than moss. The catalogue is open and shows the sandal and gives all the pertinent information. A background photo completes the spring out-of-doors setting that is suggested by the moss on the floor of the shadow box window.

The winner and still champion is the Turnbull and Asser robe in the Bergdorf Store for Men (D). The over-scaled graphic sketch in a gauche of red, black and grays is of two boxers slugging it out while the form in the background, with the red paisley silk robe — opened to show off the silky striped boxer shorts — has taken off its gloves. It knows a winner when it wears one — so what's there to fight about?

C

A&B: **Gucci, Fifth Ave., New York, NY**
James Knight, Corporate Director of Visual Presentation

C: **Sims, Ltd., Minneapolis, MN**
Mike Vye, Display Director

D: **Bergdorf, Store for Men, Fifth Ave., New York, NY**
George Shimko, Visual Director of Mens Store

D

A

A: Saks Fifth Ave., New York, NY
    William Viets, Vice President of Visual Merchandising

B&C: Lord & Taylor, Fifth Ave., New York, NY
      Alan Petersen, Vice President of Visual Merchandising and
              Store Design
      William Conard, Director of New York Windows

B

Think Mother's Day and you think of ribbons and lace — old fashioned greeting cards — flowers (espe cially pink carnations and roses) — faded pictures and silhouettes — Victorian furniture, frames and memora- bilia — wicker chairs and tables — music boxes — cameos — pearls and all those teary songs like Mother O'Mine and M is for the Million — etc. Here are some pink, pretty and particularly lovely displays catering to today's mother that are just touched with nostalgia.

The mother in Saks' display (A) in her pale pink gown sits before a matchstick blind — partially rolled down — in an antique chair. The floor is textured with muted toned pieces of slate. An urn carries an exuberant burst of cherry blossom branches — in bloom touched with green leaves and a pair of birds in the wire cage on the floor are whis- tling Mother's Day tunes.

C

P ink and lace — wide brimmed hats, bows, gloves and pieces of "antique" jewelry; they are collected in the rosy, yet shadow filled L&T (B) shadow box window as a treasure trove of other than lingerie gifts for mother. The rear wall is covered with pink fabric and yards of lace fabric are draped over it. Pink moire taffeta eddies about on the floor of the window accented with lacy ribbons.

A rather updated "hen party" takes over the pink-warmed vignette setting at L&T (C). These young mothers in their stylish lingerie are sitting in a make-believe room; a piece of molding becomes a mantle and supports a framed floral print and some miniature vases with flowers while the gravel-covered floor contrasts with the soft and silky garments and the throw pillows on it. Also see Lingerie (p. 118-119).

A

B

More for Mother. The richly cluttered settings (A&B) were part of Kaufmann's Mother's Day promotion. In both displays, pictured here, pink satin tie-back drapes frame the displays adding a sense of intimacy — and also a voyeur-ish look into a very boudoirish setting filled with ornate pieces of period furniture, vases filled with seasonal flowers and an assortment of gift ideas arranged on the floor and the tops of the furniture. The realistic mannequins show off the robes and lingerie while the framed pictures and ribbon tied gift boxes add to the feminine Mother's Day ambience.

In a much more contemporary vein are these two displays — (C&D). The Fendi display (C) features today's active mothers in a variety of separates in navy and white, and a selection of bags that compete with yet complement the many life-like babies in the display. The mother, up front, is on the go and carries her child papoose-style on her back. As a reminder of all the things Mother always told us and that we are sure to tell our children — the Mother's Commandments are inscribed on the tall front glass.

Be home before midnight
An apple a day keeps the doctor aw
Never take candy from a stranger
A penny saved is a penny earned
f you keep making that face it will stay t
Eat all your vegetables
Sleep tight-Don't let the bed bugs bi
All that glitters is not gold
Coffee will stunt your g

C

A&B: **Kaufmann's, Pittsburgh, PA**
      David Knouse, Vice President of Visual Merchandising

C: **Fendi, Fifth Ave., New York, NY**

D: **Macy's, Herald Square, New York, NY**

The Macy display (D) is a far cry from the pastels and pale lace. The stylish moms are dressed in hot pink and turquoise satin short robes over sexy lingerie. Hot pink ribbons tie up the shiny black boxes on the floor which also serve as risers for the toiletries and cologne. The sophisticated black accent appears again on the striped wallpaper over the black molding and as frames around the be-ribboned, old fashioned cut-out silhouettes we remember from old time Mother's day displays.

D

We introduced Navy as part of our review of Cruise/Resort wear and showed how Navy teamed up with red and with yellow — plus white for Nautical themes. On these pages we show a variety of dresses, suits, and separates all in navy or navy and white, and how the designers at Bergdorf Goodman treated them at different times. The Bergdorf signature look is apparent throughout and though each display is different — they are all done with the style that is decidedly Bergdorf.

(A) sends out a message that needs to be decoded. The long panel on the left combines letters and numbers in a decorative graphic design while the cartoon-style balloon floating between the mannequins in navy and the one in white does yield up the information that Jr. Suits are on 2.

B: Star struck and somewhat nautical. Six pointed stars are sponged on the rear white wall and on the front glass sandwiching the navy suited mannequin between them. A candelabra/applique with a big brass star all but hides the mannequin's face but it does bring the viewer right up to the main reason for this navy story.

B

A

C

A,B,C,D: Bergdorf Goodman, Fifth Ave., New York, NY
Richard Currier, Vice President of Visual
Presentation

D

CFollowing in the footsteps of top fashion — or just learning the newest dance craze, the three red haired mannequins are enveloped in a swirl of right feet and left feet and all the connecting dashes that help to explain the steps. The navy suits are washed with warm light and some of the foot movements are purposefully lost in the deep shadows overhead.

D: In a decorative cityscape: a plan view of the streets that run north and south — east and west as well as vertical projections, all askew, are some of the buildings that fill in the white blocks between the black streets. The red arrow on top locates Bergdorf Goodman and miniature autos, busses and trucks in primary colors defy gravity as they ride over the vertical street grid. As in the other Bergdorf displays — some of the angled skyscrapers are painted on the front glass putting the mannequins in the middle of the artwork. Note how few and how simple the props are that are used in the Bergdorf displays and how much depends upon artwork and improvisation.

nna Karan on 2

A

B

Navy suits and separates: navy striped and patterned. The sexy, Donna Karan navy, pin striped suit with lace trimmed slip showing in Saks stylish window (A) is classy, classic and contemporary. It contrasts with the ornate, carved Grinling Gibbons-like frames and the 17th cent. portraits of English royalty — after the Reformation. The painting provides the "romance" of yesterday and the all-white, stark setting is totally "today."

Gucci (B) plays up their navy trimmed with white bags and shoes in this neutral setting. Against the rear wall and haloed with light are two semi-abstracts wearing navy and white suits and carrying coats. The three blue and white patterned pedestals, up front, in their own light show off the color coordinated accessories with a single dash of color on the scarf that is draped over the central bag.

C

acy's (C) takes the Adrienne Vittadini navy and white knit separates down to the seashore and the clear vinyl shower curtain printed with assorted white sea shells is hung from above by pieces of white cord. The floor and back wall are white and the copy across the front glass is in navy blue.

Lord & Taylor (D) teams up navy and white with stripes and dots. The setting, like the composition, is classic; a black and gold pedestal supports a piece of sculpture on an ingenious gilt base and another sculpture — African style — rests on the floor near the seated mannequin in the striped jacket. The two standing figures wear trousers with the striped pattern that leads the viewer's eye down to the henna headed mannequin on the floor. Her bent knees bring the eye up towards the standing figures — and the composition has made a complete circuit. Note the mottled "sky" on the rear wall created by the filtered lights and the shadows.

A: Saks Fifth Ave., New York, NY
    William Viets, Vice President of Visual Merchandising

B: Gucci, Fifth Ave., New York, NY
    James Knight, Corporate Director of Visual Presentations

C: Macy's, Herald Square, New York, NY

D: Lord & Taylor, Fifth Ave., New York, NY
    Alan Petersen, Vice President Store Design/Visual
        Merchandising
    William Conard, Director of New York Windows

D

A

When cool winds blow — when summer gives way to fall and signs of winter begin to appear — it is time for outerwear promotions which used to be, not too long ago, the Coat & Suit promotions of August. But this Outerwear is more costume — more re-laxed and easy, and more for the country rather than city streets.

Under Import (p. 105) we introduced Liberty of London's Ireland promotion. Here (A) you can feel the cold and chilling winds coming in off the sea — climbing the craggy, stone strewn shore and enveloping these abstract mannequins layered, wrapped and swaddled in luxurious wool scarves and shawls against the unfriendly weather. The low keyed light plays against the streaked gray wall, the textured rough gray rocks and stones, and creates the chilling ambience while the figures are warmed by the reds and golds of their woolen coverings.

A: **Liberty of London, London, England**
Paul Muller, Director of Sales Promotions and Visual Presentation

B: **Gucci, Fifth Ave., New York, NY**
James Knight, Corporate Director of Visual Presentations

C: **Hirshleifer's, Manhasset, NY**
Design by IDEAS

B

Gucci presents its quilted black coat (B) in a sub
dued, outdoors setting. A few birch logs stretched
horizontally across the window become a rustic
fence for the semi-abstract, white mannequin to sit on. A gold
Gucci scarf is tied around her head and a light picks out the
animal print bag and the quilted pattern of the jacket.

The same black/gold combination was used in the
Hirshleifer display (C). The quilted 3/4 length coat is more
dressy — as is the black and gold trimmed outfit on the
companion. The gray quilted coat is enhanced by the gold
colored scarf and the felt slouch hat. Literally framing the
figures in the dark space is the rustic twig arch that stands
on the wood chip covered floor. Orange jack-o-lantern
foliage is woven into the rough twig frame adding a gentle
touch of fall color.

C

A

A: Barneys, Seventh Ave., New York, NY
Simon Doonan, Senior Vice President Advertising/Display
Steven Johanknecht, Director of Windows

B: Saks Fifth Ave., New York, NY
William Viets, Vice President of Visual Merchandising

C: Macy's, Herald Square, New York, NY

D: Fendi, Fifth Ave., New York, NY

B

Putting the Sport in outer SPORTSwear: bringing hobbies and sports activities into the window to help sell to the targeted customer. This Barneys window (A) was one of a surreal set of windows that combined unlikely, everyday objects in decorative all-over patterns on the rear wall with the fashionable outerwear up front. This leather coat is surrounded by dozens of black rubber boots and yellow telephones. Are you getting a message? A black hat is raised into prominence on a tall black stand. What is it? Is it part of the message — or is there a message? Does it really matter? If you know your shoppers and you know what they like — what amuses them — what intrigues them — then go for it. Barneys does!

Saks does it in a more traditional manner; with textures and colors. The formal wood rear wall of the window is lost behind the applied twigs and branches that suggest either a reed fence or a thicket. Adding to the outdoors ambience and the rich fall colors is the Native American woven carpet on the floor full of orange, beiges and browns. The suit form is layered and the non-existent hand holds a russet colored leather cap — the same color as the shoes tucked under the pants that are hung from the waist of the form.

Think sport — think Polo — thing Graphics. The creamy white Macy's window (C) sports a headless form really dressed to take on the slopes — the snow and even the apres ski drinks around a roaring fire. The jacketed figure on the right is opened up to reveal the many layers worn beneath. On the wall — not hung but just resting on the molding strip across the back — a variety of snowscapes and winter sports scenes all in simple frames of assorted sizes.

The Fendi ladies are also dressed for the slopes and since they wouldn't think of traveling without their Fendi luggage, some of the pieces are being chairlifted into the upper reaches of the tall window. Also up and away are the skis and ski poles which, like in the Macy's display, sets the time and place. But who needs ice and snow to know where these headless forms are heading when they look so at home in the warm glow of the space.

C

D

A

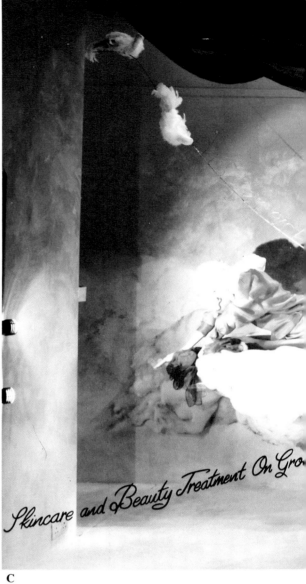

C

B

A: Marshall Field's, Chicago, IL
Jamie Becker, State St. Window Director

B: Macy's, Herald Square, New York, NY

C: Harvey Nichols, London, England
Mary Portas, Head of Sales Promotion and Visual
Presentation

Perfumes, cosmetics and toiletries are small and often precious things that are usually presented in large fashion windows. As discussed in Accessories, ideally they need small, intimate and, yes, precious spaces like shadow boxes but with strong vibrant color, risers and platforms, and over-scaled settings or props to envelop them so they can succeed in the larger windows.

(A) Marshall Field's "Red" promotion couldn't be more emphatic; from the RED logo on the front glass to the realistic mannequin in the vibrant red gown — to the ribbon be-decked gold wire candle holders carrying RED boxes instead of candles on top — to the actual display of RED perfume on the stand in front of the mannequin. The product presentation is backed up by a red and gold patterned heart. The sharp lighting picks out the products but the viewer is only too willing to come and look for them herself.

The Image is Calvin Klein and there is no doubt that the viewer will recognize the promotion. The TV monitor replays the latest TV "Escape" commercials — and the cool, serene look of the wood paneled back wall and the contemporary black lacquered table are pure Klein as is the gray outfit on the mannequin. Almost up at the glass is a display of "Escape" on a build-up of light-colored leather luggage. Another array of products is set out on the table between the figure and the TV monitor. The tall exotic plant serves as a flag over the arrangement. On the rear wall are fashion photos of models in Klein designs.

Harvey Nichols (C) dares to be different — and shocking — and unique in its corner location in Knightsbridge. This most unexpected display has a mannequin in a pale blue robe floating on a tulle puffed cloud and a less than beautiful face sticks out from behind the gold wreath coyly and cutely decorated with gilded cherubs and mermaids. Blue swags are draped from above and the rear wall and floor are tinted with blue lights. What's it all about? The message on the glass — on the left — says "Skincare and Beauty Treatments on Ground."

A

E

B

A&B: P.A. Bergner, Milwaukee, WI
      Charles Luckenbill, Vice President of Visua
      Merchandising

C,D,E: Marshall Field's, Chicago, IL
        Jamie Becker, State St. Window Director
        Amy Meadows, Window Manager

For the promotion of Dune perfume in its new coral and gold packaging Bergner's window (A) feature some over-scaled white sea shells; over-scaled to attract attention to the white sand-covered floor and the Dune perfumes, colognes, and toiletries displayed there. Tying the composition together and enhancing the color of the packaging is the coral swag of fabric that starts above the viewer's eye level and works its way down to spread out on the floor around one of the large sea shells and the merchandise arranged near it.

C

D

The Davidoff's Cool Water men's cologne promotion (B) made extensive use of the Cool Water ad and graphics that appeared in the better men's and women's fashion magazines because here the appeal is to women. Between the graphics there are gift boxes topped with the toiletries arranged in bands across the rear wall and the angled side partitions. The two pedestals, front and center, also showed an assortment of Cool Water products — up near eye level.

Curlicue wire armatures painted gold and topped with bouquets of assorted pink flowers are set in the glowing red Marshall Field's window (C) to introduce the new Narcisse perfume from Chloe. Up front and closer to the glass, on a lower wire scrolled stand is a gift package display of the new product.

Safari (D) gets a shadow box treatment at MF and the graphics from the magazine ad and animal print accessories are combined with the Ralph Lauren products. The many size boxes become elevations for the perfumes and colognes and spilling over from the travel trunk is a spray of fabric that eddies in and around the boxes, bottles and costume jewelry — engulfing them all.

The Lancome promotion at MF (E) relied on the oversized black dominoes to reach from above eye level down to the presentation of the product at floor level. They capture the viewer's eye as they tumble forward in the space. On the lowest domino is a lay-down of the toiletries and the graphics pertaining to them. As in several of the other displays, the oversized props help to bring attention to the products.

A

B

P rints and patterns — fields of flowers or landscapes of lines or dots, soft subdued colors or colors clashing and bursting with energy. Each season seems to bring its own prints — its own patterns — its own palette of colors and on these next few pages we present some of the myriad variations on the theme.

Floral print dresses are cropping up in the Marshall Field's windows (A&B) and they are presented on stylized mannequins set in a black window. Lighting up the scene — literally as well as figuratively — are the lamp shades suspended down on coiled copper wires or on copper candlesticks capped with leaf-trimmed shades. Sprays and corsages of spring flowers decorate the imbricated green shades layered with tier after tier of green leaves, overlapping that glow with light.

Daffy's toys with the flowers that bloom in the spring (C) by having the very stylized figures sprouting an assortment of tulips rising out of their top knots. The background is a soft, cloud-filled sky, and ornamental plastic fencing zigzags across the window involving the mannequins in their spring finery prints accented with yellows and coral.

C

D

Print dresses are on the agenda at Lord & Taylor (D) and to stress the point, they title this sunny setting "America's Dress Address." A few white garden chairs and a fantasy figure sculpted in topiary by "Edward Scissorhands" makes the scene. The topiary is dressed in a print of flowers — like the prints on the dresses. The center figure in yellow gets the full sunlight treatment which pours in from the left. The background is mottled in yellow gold/ochre and sits back in the shadows. A few additional flower pots with flowering plants are added for interest — and balance.

A

A: Elizabeth Arden, Fifth Ave., New York, NY
   Noel MacFetrich, Display Director

B: Laura Ashley, E. 57th St., New York, NY
   Barbara Kleber, Corp., Director of Visual Merchandising

C: Escada, E. 57th St., New York, NY
   Gregory Khoury, Display Director

D: La Grande Dame, Puerto Rico
   Frank Caballero, Designer

B

Polka dots and stripes — plaids and Mondrian patterns — spring, summer and fall; it all depends upon the colors. Polka dots — like Navy Blue — is a sure sign of spring, and at Elizabeth Arden (A) the dots are white on bright chrome yellow. The setting in this open back window couldn't be simpler or better: a panel of black fabric dotted with white semi-divides the space and the floor board is covered with a reverse of the fabric. The spindly black chair is upholstered in the yellow to match the dress. Geoffrey Beene gets "credit" with cut-out white letters sitting on a black plaque.

Laura Ashley (B) treats its summery black and white dotted dress with a "modiste" setting. The tri-part screen suggests a little dress shop — right out of the Victorian period — with ruffled curtains and a draped dress form painted on the screen. The foreground of the shallow window has the dressed dress form sharing the space with assorted striped and dotted hat boxes — some white straw hats and black satin ribbons. One ribbon is tied as a bow at the neck of the form and a few well chosen spots and dashes of coral spice up the smart black and white display.

C

D

Stained glass or Mondrian? The suit in the Escada window (C) is boxed off in navy/black and each box is filled with either soft yellow, pale orange, or light or medium blue. Similar blocks of color are tacked onto the black back wall of the space. In addition to the light on the realistic mannequins, there is another light targeted on the accessory grouping rising up from the black floor pad on a gilt stand.

La Grande Dame (D) breaks out in boxes too — but these are black and white checkerboard patterns of assorted sizes pieced and patched together — then subdued by the white pants. The setting is all white and the old desk has been playfully painted in black and white, and like the tunic top, trimmed with spots and slashes of clear red. The chair, also abstractly painted in black and white and accented with red, takes to the ceiling in an attention getting upside down position. Adding to the enigma of it all are the "S" or "5" shapes floating on the white walls.

A

B

C

Bright, bold, bountiful and beautiful blasts of color — prints that dazzle — bewilder and bewitch — camouflage and confuse — that reach out and take over. Interestingly, when the prints and patterns are strong, the backgrounds are often just as powerful; taming the foreground by overplaying the background.

The wild and wonderful French prints at Galeries Lafayette (A) are worn by a pair of realistic — hardly over the top — mannequins. Even the polychromatic background, very strong in color and pattern, is remarkably neat, orderly and controlled. A great and inexpensive "graphic" idea for a background is the arrangement of the dozens of post cards with reproductions of famous paintings — available in most museums or card stores.

Harvey Nichols (B) returns to the '70s — with this mix and unmatched collection of Dolce y Gabbana "costumes" accented with plumed hats and second hand store accessories. On the back wall, white washed LP records float like champagne bubbles in the pink ambience. Up front, on the floor — the music lingers on with a selection of old-time (at least 25 years old) record players also sprayed dead white for contrast to the print and patterned clothes.

The designer's name, Todd Oldham, made up of fanciful letters soars over the boldly-striped wall with more colors than decorated Joseph's techni-colored coat. The separates gathered in the Bendel window (C) on black abstracts is a varied selection of patterns. The copy scrawled in black on the window is an open invitation to "mingle and blend" or "scramble and separate" the Oldham separates.

D

A: **Galeries Lafayette, E. 57th St., New York, NY**

B: **Harvey Nichols, London, England**
   Mary Portas, Head of Sales Promotion and Visual
   Merchandising

C: **Henri Bendel, Fifth Ave., New York, NY**
   Barbara Putnam, Display Director

D: **Macy's, Herald Square, New York, NY**

Another toast to the Hippie culture of the late-'60s-early-'70s is the Macy display (D). The mannequins — male and female — all have long lank hair with bandanas tied around their foreheads and they have the fringed and tattered look of the "Woodstock" generation. A giant peace symbol trimmed with pieces of flags and bandana prints fills the background while "mushrooms" pop up from the pattern washed floor. For those who were part of that celebration — this is a nostalgia filled window. For those too young to have been there — but follow the Grateful Dead — the music lingers on.

A

B

Rain, rain don't go away — I'm all dressed in Burberry today. When you are Burberry — or when you own a Burberry you almost look forward to the clouds and the gentle rain that falls from heaven — because you know you are blessed with the best in rainwear. You are not only protected — you are in style and fashionably correct. On these pages are some of the different approaches to a drippy subject made bright and almost sunny.

A sense of humor certainly does not hurt and the realistic ladies in red and orange coats are in the good company of the worldwide recognized Burberry plaid umbrellas. The slashing strings of silvery wire that suggest the rain are carrying dozens of little paper parasols — the kind one usually finds stuck in an exotic fruity drink. "It's not raining rain you know — it's raining rain stoppers."

However, in the men's display (B) it is raining the proverbial "cats and dogs" though the cats and dogs are miniature plastic reproductions. Some animal lovers might be offended by seeing life-like, stuffed toy animals hurtling through space but who can be upset by these colorful toy things on the streams of light-catching wire diagonally pulled through the space with the coats shown on suit forms? Here, too, the umbrellas play their part.

A,B,C,D: Burberry's, E. 57th St., New York, NY
Michael Stewart, Display Director

D

A color statement is made in (C). The camel, red and black of the Burberry plaid gets a big presentation number on a series of wood-topped and wood-based forms. Red scarves and sweaters add flair and furled panache while several other Burberry plaid accessories are introduced. The expert draping and shaping of the coats and accessories fills the black space with movement and vitality.

Breaking through the yellow clouds of summer (D) is this classic red Burberry coat topped with the equally classic Burberry scarf. Red umbrellas carry the sale message and light breaks through from between the cut-out foam board clouds — heralding a bright new day and the awaited event.

A

B

A: **Lord & Taylor, Fifth Ave., New York, NY**
William Conard, Director of New York Windows

B: **Gigi, Munich, Germany**
Peter Rank Design

C: **Place Desjardins, Montreal, Que., Canada**
Decors Yves Guilbeault, Inc.
Andre Doyon, Photographer

Red, hot and wonderful. We have already seen red used as a strong accent with black — as a patriotic addition to navy and white — and here is Red doing its own thing.

The realistic mannequins in L&T's window (A) are leaning against an art nouveau, whiplash lined balustrade and looking down into the lowest level of the L&T elevator window. The floor is neutrally tiled in gray and white squares and even the textured wall is gray. The red dresses and accessories are tied in with the photo enlargement of the open red rose in the frame with the undulating border. A single red rose was dropped on the floor. Red light washes over the gray surfaces and also stops to enhance the color of the dresses.

Gigi (B) features dressy suits of red-violet on stylized white mannequins in a black setting enriched with squares of gold leaf. The mannequins' wigs and make-up are also done with gold leaf and black is the accent color for one of the suits. The bouquet of dried red roses held by the seated mannequin has fallen apart and some flowers now lie on the natural wood floor.

For the fall presentation of new suits at Place Desjardins (C), the display designer selected a hot, sizzling, analogous palette of red, red/orange and red/violet/cerise — accented with gold. To tell the suit story the setting is vivid red — almost as vivid and vibrant as the outfits and the feathery accessories. A small red upholstered chaise lounge and some gilded brackets on the wall "set the scene" and the strong dramatic lighting finishes it all off. The faces of the very stylized mannequins are accented with light — to get attention for the attention-getting outfits.

C

A

A: Ungaro, Madison Ave., New York, NY
Marc Manigault, Designer

B: Willowbrook Mall, Wayne, NJ
Design: Jeri Lugo and Glenn Sokoli

C: Liberty of London, London, England
Paul Muller, Director of Promotions and Visual Presentation

D: Saks Fifth Ave., New York, NY
William Viets, Vice President of Visual Merchandising

Red — red prints — red plaids — all mixed together under the watchful eye of the red lacquered classic bust perched on top of an equally red pedestal. Sitting on the red floor pad is another red bust — blindfolded with a black satin ribbon. The black in the costumes is teamed up with the black ribbon streamers that also tie up the group of figures into an effective composition.

Another joint effort (see Malls) is this red promotion at Willowbrook Mall (B). Black fabric covers the large central cube and the amoeba-shaped platforms below it. To complement as well as further the "red" promotion, giant roses constructed out of foam board are used to prop the display area. All the mannequins are accessorized with belts that dangle black letters that spell out "Willowbrook."

B

D

C

G etting a real look at red teamed with black — through the shot and shattered slats of the white blinds in the all-white Liberty of London window (C). The sharp red jackets and shirts are teamed up with black and a single print tie cascades out of the breast pocket of the jacket. On the floor: the shell-shocked remains of the slats that didn't make it — but that does make it possible for the viewer on the street to get the intriguing, see-through view into the window.

Whether it's a horse of another color — or if it's a different stripe, the almost life-like zebra stands tethered, front and center, in this Saks window (D) aglow with steamy red and amber light. The titian haired, realistic mannequin in the red ball gown rests against the patient zebra. The designers used the animal as a draw; to bring the viewer closer to follow up with an inspection of the elegant gown that is almost casually shown behind the zebra.

A sale is a many splendored thing; it can be elegantly understated — it can be a message pummeled home by constant repetition — it can be spelled out, suggested, turned into a fun event. It can be the wrath of an angry retailer brought down on the unsuspecting heads of shoppers. To show off only a few of the myriad ways to make the best of merchandise that didn't sell — and how to say Sale in any language — the following.

January is Sale month in Paris and it seems like a National "holiday" since all the windows — from the top designers and boutiques to the department store and popular-priced shops do it — and they do it up with the soignee style suitable to the store's image.

Daniel Hechter (A) shows off a pair of white dress forms dressed only in lavender satin ribbon and not a single garment is on view in the white window. The simple black "Soldes" (sale) message is applied to the white seamless paper rolled down against the rear wall.

Phillipe Adec (B) has its dress form wrapped like a mummy in red tissue paper and then secured with black satin ribbon. The drop light in the window fully illuminates the form and the red and black "solde" sign unfurled before the form. The magazine ads below let the shopper know what to expect in the sale.

Zapa (C) puts white plastic garment bags over their dress forms — ties them at the bottom and the applied letters spell out the by-now familiar message. In the three French examples no merchandise was actually shown; each one — in one way or another — made use of the dress forms that are their stock-in-trade — their signatures — and the Soldes story was related with style and discretion.

Marky Mark of the Calvin Klein underwear ads and also the rapper with the bulging pecs takes over the North Beach Leather display (D) for a Marky-Mark-down sale. If you don't know who Marky Marks is — you will recognize the body, and if not the face — at least the baseball cap.

A: **Daniel Hechter, Paris**

B: **Phillipe Adec, Paris**

C: **Zapa, Paris**

D&E: **North Beach Leather, Boston, MA**
Kristin Lauer, Blue Potato, Boston

A

B

C

D

E

I f once is enough — how much more emphatic is it if the message is repeated in neat, orderly rows — in black and white — accented with red frames on a white wall? The designer took this sale promotion (E) on the road and simulated license plates with the framed signs sparked with reflectors. Of course, the road theme was inspired by the leather jacket with the stop signs and the broken white line that divides the highway — or the yoke of the jacket. Even the reclining figure has an octagonal stop sign appliqued on her tank top. AND — it is all in red, white and black! It's subtle — but obvious; direct but detoured with taste.

A

B

A: **Burberry, E. 57th St., New York, NY**
Michael Stewart, Display Director

B&C: **Charles Jourdan, Trump Tower, New York, NY**
David Griffin, Display Director

D: **Henri Bendel, Fifth Ave., New York, NY**
Barbara Putnam, Display Director

E: **Zegna, Fifth Ave., New York, NY**

C

S pelling it all out in red, white and black — or even
just black and white. A real balancing act: the dress
form dressed in gray and topped with a red hat and
coat in the Burberry window (A) appears to be stepping
forward from the totally red environment around her. The
lights catch a glimpse of the Burberry signature plaid scarf
— the small articulated wooden figure on the floor with a
message banner — and the main attraction, the pile of
white gift boxes frothing with white excelsior and embellished with red letters spelling out the occasion. Also see
Rainwear p. 173.

Charles Jourdan also did it with red, white and black. In (B) a black and white graphic of a shopper from the '50s with her shopping bag accentuated in red steps forward from the red fabric panel that slides down the rear (to close off the open back window) and across to the front glass. In the chromed supermarket cart there is a red Jourdan shopping bag, shoe boxes, shoes, bags and black and white catalogues. Barely seen on the far right is a gray step displayer with shoes in red and black shown on the various levels.

The striped red and white fabric in (C) carries the strong Sale sign and a white fabric drape cuts diagonally across the wall to bring attention to the red shopping bags, boxes, handbags, and shoes displayed on the red/white striped floor pad. In both of the Jourdan windows red and black merchandise was featured to emphasize the sale color scheme though other colored merchandise was available inside.

E

D

Bendel's (D) does its Sale with style and chic. The white mannequins wear white terry robes each monogrammed with one letter of the magic word. Their heads are wrapped with soaring turbans of terrycloth and the polka dotted triangles and the black and white striped fabric on the rear wall are meant to suggest cabanas or bath houses. To complete the summer sale setting, the figures stand ankle deep in white sand.

(E) Tattoos that make a difference. The muscular chests of the shiny black forms carry the story in white for all to read in this carefully-lit window. Everything is black and the sale letters drift up from all that darkness to do their thing with polish and elan.

A

B

C

A,B,C: Hugo Boss, Washington, DC
   Display by PROP: John Kiser

D: Barneys, Manhasset, NY
   Simon Doonan, Senior Vice President Advertising/Display

E: Escada, E. 57th St., New York, NY

E

The Hugo Boss shop in Washington knows how to throw a sale. Their windows are always clever, amusing, usually devoid of merchandise and in stark black and white with yellow or gold accents. In no way do they ever put down their sale garments — or the customers who want to buy them. Hugo Boss sells style and thus their sales have that same sense of style and class.

(A&C) took measure of the sale promotion by playing up and playing with the yellow tape measure. These tailor's tapes were used to drape around the black fabric suit forms or to tie up a black chair or the white background panel. Stenciled tape measure markings — greatly overstated — add a sophisticated graphic element to the coordinated displays as did the simple sale card in white which dangles around the necks of the forms or get caught up in the tape measure web on the chair. In another Hugo Boss sale event (B) things were going for a song — and the display carried the tune. Music sheets, large music notes and a real gilt music stand replayed the theme along with the sheet music from "Going My Way" with Bing Crosby's picture on it. Any way you looked at the window — the merchandise was going — the sale way.

D

Barneys (D) had a breakthrough sale and the mes sage on the wall behind the fallout of bricks is a subtle sale sign — certainly no Mene Mene Tekel. The pile of bricks, on the floor, neatly pulls the debris together. The stylized white mannequin in the gray suit in the neutral setting is elegant and calm considering what happened behind him.

On target. Escada (E) says it with a bull's eye target in black and white and a black dress form decorated with hundreds of "E"s in gold. The angled arrows rising off the white floor also take the viewer down to the message in white on white that says that there is a sale in progress. It's forceful — it's direct and yet it has refinement

A

C

B

A: Macy's, Herald Square, New York, NY

B: Hirshleifer, Manhasset, NY
   Display by IDEAS

C: Harvey Nichols, London, England
   Mary Portas, Head of Sales Promotion and Visual
       Merchandising

eparates: the many parts that are designed to go together — to be mixed — to be matched — to be offered as options — as alternatives — as extras to stretch a basic wardrobe. Sometimes it is a print and a solid combined in a variety of tops, jackets, skirts and pants — or it is a color scheme — or a print that needs a solid or a solid-looking for a matching print. Throughout this book we have included many Separates displays under a variety of headings but here we pick just a few for special consideration.

The Macy's window (A) offers black, black and white, yellow, and orange in an assortment of separates that can be combined or entwined. The surreal black and white background adds familiar and unfamiliar objects — not necessarily related — in a decorative scheme. The three black slats that rise up from the floor carry a red shoe, a candelabra and a black hat adorned with white satin

domino masks. The black ribbon "shadows" on the floor add some diagonal lines to the design.

Hirshleifer (B) combines a vest and jacket of the same print with a compatible print shirt along with the black pants, hat and shoes in this artistic setting. The background is a cartoon-y line design in black and white within a big black mat and a gold leafed frame resting on an easel. The sketch recalls the graphic design of the print being featured.

The fractured faces — the floating physiognomy are all blow-up Fornasetti designs. The all-black-and-white Harvey Nichols window (C) shows off some all-black garments that can be re-assembled into assorted costumes. Xeroxed in black and white are magazine covers which are used to paper the bases on which the dress forms are elevated and a Fornasetti sun face hides the fact that the form is headless.

A

The rich earthy fall colors make an appearance on this page with jackets, coats, skirts, sweaters, and blouses that are all ready to play "change partners" — and separates. A few weathered artifacts set the scene in Aquascutum (A) which is then filled to overflowing with dried foliage; the floor is piled high with drifts of autumn leaves while clusters of dried hydrangeas erupt from the planter — all in subdued colors. An amber light suffuses the rear wall.

Gucci (B) shows them in colored coordinates and with some taste and imagination and any of these scarves or leather accessories — these tops and bottoms could be rearranged with the prints of the scarves providing "the raison d'etre." The dress forms are elevated on the slat topped table and assorted fashion accessories are hung off the pegs extending out from the wood molding that runs around the neutral space. Here, too, the burst of fall foliage in the rear ties the fall palette together.

The Kenzo separates were meant for each other and as shown behind the broken blind in Liberty of London (C) the hot pink jacket and skirt could come together as a smart suit — or become shocking companions for the vibrant prints. How they go together is shown but it is up to the individual shopper to figure out how she will team them up and when she'll wear them.

B

C

A: **Aquascutum, Fifth Ave., New York, NY**
   Display by IDEAS

B: **Gucci, Fifth Ave., New York, NY**
   James Knight, Corporate Director of Visual Presentation

C: **Liberty of London, London, England**
   Paul Muller, Director of Promotions and Visual Presentation

A

B

C

Way back at the beginning of this book we intro duced the all-important Fashion Accessories that will "make" or "date" an outfit. We did show some shoes along with bags but since shoes are such an important element in a costume we have devoted several pages for a look down — onto the floor — to see how to bring shoes up into view.

A cut-out crocodile makes its way across the Gucci window (A) and it carries a procession of red reptile textured shoes on its back. Sitting inside the open mouth is another shoe but it is the boot caught in the mouth that gets the smile. A yellow light warms up the curved white wall and it casts a warm glow over the red shoes raised up on the cut out wooden ripples.

You could get a boot out of this L&T display (B) as the styrofoam snow spills over from one beautiful boot into the other. White fabric, spun glass, crystal snowflakes, and icy lace patterns on the glass all together create the winter wonderland feeling.

The canvas bags trimmed with leather not only elevate the leather sandals in the Ann Taylor shadow box window (C) — one of the bags also holds the giant sunflower and the wispy foliage. They not only complement the rich tawny leather, they set the time and place for these summery fashion accessories.

D

A: **Gucci, Fifth Ave., New York, NY**
   James Knight, Corporate Director of Visual Presentation

B: **Lord & Taylor, Fifth Ave., New York, NY**
   William Conard, Director of Fifth Ave. Windows

C: **Ann Taylor, E. 57th St., New York, NY**

D: **Frivola, Puerto Rico**
   Frank Caballero, Designer

Frivola (D) combines different elements and ideas in this open back window. Raised to eye level is a piece of checkerboard floor with a gray styro arcade jutting out of the classic gold frame. A piece of blue sky is still captured in the frame. Another piece of the "puzzle" — sky and arcade with steps sits on the right with some shoes located on it. The black and white checkerboard panel makes a short dividing wall around the window and other styles and colors of shoes are shown on white covered rectangles. The MR16 lights — suspended down from above provide the brilliant accent light for the shoes being shown.

A

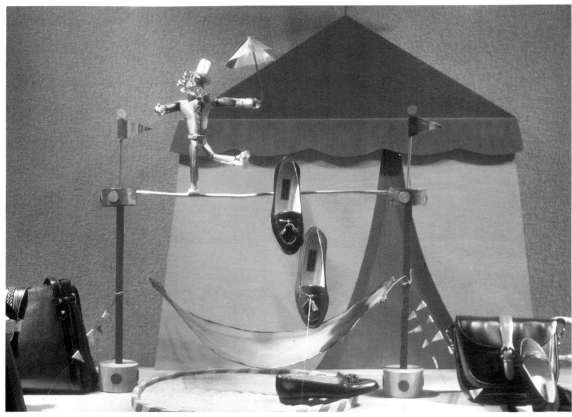

B

A&B: **Cole Haan, Madison Ave., New York, NY**
       Judy Hamlin, Corporate Director of Visuals
       Justin & Larabee, Designers

C,D,E: **Gucci, Fifth Ave., New York, NY**

C

D

E

E ven shoe stores develop their signature looks and some of these identifiable styles are shown on these pages and those that follow.

Cole Haan — an International group of fine leather shops makes use of unique props and clever elevations to show off their fine merchandise in the New York store. A blue/gray textured panel (A) carries a deeper blue frame and a painting of daubs of ochre and yellow paints. The old chair is painted Pompeiian red and it carries a few shoes — casually arranged. This men's display includes some leather briefcases and carry-on pieces, shoes, belts, ties, suspenders and socks — all sort of organized on the pale yellow floor.

The circus has made it to town (B) and it's a sure sign of spring. The tinker toy constructions are just right in scale for the shadow box window they appear in. The tin man acrobat with matching umbrella performs over the center ring along with the star performer — a pair of shoes. Other shoes and bags are arranged in this space with the cut out and applied circus tent on the rear wall.

A look of another kind for another purveyor of fine leather fashions and accessories: Gucci. A series of flat cut out disks (C) subtly rendered to suggest dimensional beach balls spill over from above eye level down to below eye level — showing off a range of colorful play shoes. The lighting is on the shoes at the different levels and then it pours over onto the neutral colored wall.

A men's shoe window (D) combines 4x4 wooden posts of assorted heights with molded bases and different colors and types of gourds displayed on top of the risers — like pieces of dimensional artwork. A single moccasin takes over one post at the eye-level position. On the white floor more shoes shuffle across all heading in the same direction.

S trips of thin wood veneer edging painted flat white are woven into these fanciful forms which actually serve to capture and show off the colorful summer flats at different eye levels. The neutral rear wall is flushed with yellow which also turns some of the strips of veneer pale yellow in the shadowy areas.

COLE · HAAN

A

A: Cole Haan, Fifth Ave., New York, NY
    Judy Hamlin, Director of Visual Displays
    Justin & Larabee, Display Designers

B&C: Signora, Munich, Germany
     Peter Rank Design

B

C

ole Haan's spring window (A) is a study in classics and textures. The back wall is a screen of creamy, unglazed tiles "mortared" with moss and more of the green moss makes an island on the wooden floor of the window. Standing on the moss is a gray marbleized Corinthian capped pedestal draped with a silvery gray fabric. Two shoes with matching bags sit atop the pedestal and other shoes and bags are casually grouped on the mossy surface. The pale straw light casts a sunny glow over the whole setting.

Three giant mache feathers are angled in the Signora window (B) and each one carries three shoes at eye level. A giant knot of natural raffia is tied around the tip of the feather and the raffia swirls forward towards the glass.

In another Signora window (C) the mannequin's top is hidden behind the open newspaper which carries the "NEWS." The message is clearly stated in black and some of the all-black merchandise is "italicized" with nail-head trim. A pair of short boots finish the stockinged legs and the piles of newspapers that fill the open back window act as elevation for the shoes, bags and boots. The lighting adds drama and pizzazz to the striking setting.

A

C

B: Sonia Rykiel, Madison Ave., New York, NY
   Marc Manigault, Designer

D: Harvey Nichols, London, England
   Mary Portas, Head of Sales Promotion and Visual
     Merchandising

E: ZCMI, Salt Lake City, UT
   Mike Stevens, Display Director
   Design Team: Sherri Orton / Anne Cook /
     Gertrude Glauser / Marcelo Zapata

Spring: the sunshine after the rain — the grass grows and the snow is gone — blue skies replace the gray ones and the buds are busting out all over. Birds are returning from wherever they have been and all is right with the world as it is once again reborn.

The sunshine of spring fills the Ferragamo window (A) and the Sonia Rykiel display space (B). Constructions of birch branches are finished with corsages of flowers and pegs to hold the fashion accessories, and they confine the fully dressed and accessorized forms in the shadow laden window. Three bark textured birdhouses are suspended over the Rykiel drapers to become the heads for the hanger-hung outfits. Some birds have taken up residence up above while others on the green seamless paper island are still looking for living and nesting quarters.

Ferragamo thinks pink for spring (C) and also thinks birdhouses will set the spring theme. In their approach the colorful birdhouses are balanced on black lacquered poles horizontally stretched across the black space and the familiar Ferragamo triangular rear wall panel is peach/pink to go with the suits on the stylized black figures.

B

E

D

You get to expect the unexpected at Harvey Nichols (D). A green tree grows horizontally across the window dividing the space in half. Green treelets defy gravity and grow at right angles to the tree. The white mannequins in their white outfits lounge about in the white space with the white gravel floor. You can feel the sunlight streaming in from the right.

As part of ZCMI's salute to the seasons they announced that early spring was a wonderful season and it is as presented in this display (E). It is also a most delicious season since it is all executed in gum-drops, jelly beans, tinted marshmallows, popcorn, and all sorts of colorful candies of various sizes and shapes. These giant-size candy mosaics were great shopper stoppers.

A

A: Lord & Taylor, Fifth Ave., New York, NY
   William Conard, Director of Fifth Ave. Windows

B: Saks Fifth Ave., New York, NY

C: ZCMI, Salt Lake City, UT
   Mike Stevens, Visual Director

Spring means gardens and gardening — wheel barrows, pots for planting, earth and moss, seed packets, rakes and hoes — and a clear blue sky with soft fleecy clouds.

The mannequin in L&T's window (A) is resting up from toiling in the fields — in her white negligee(?) — and she's soaking up some of the yellow light that fills the window. She rests against a weathered wood trough filled with flowers, bushes and terra cotta pots for planting. On the white wall — supported on brackets fashioned out of lattice wood grids are more pots, rakes, hoes and sprouting plants.

Another reclining figure appears in Saks window (B) in a yellow and pink dress. In this all-white window, blue clouds float over the chalk sky and giant yellow sunflowers grow out of the white pot which is tinted with the pink light leads into the diagonal pose of the mannequin.

Springtime brights take to the road at ZCMI. Diagonals slash across the space in strong colors; triangles — arrows — and oblique rectangles. Even the message on the glass travels across the display — on an angle in a dynamic frame that suggests movement.

B

TRAVELING BRIGHT

C

A

A: Galeries Lafayette, E. 57th St., New York, NY

B: Bloomingdales, Lexington Ave., New York, NY

C&D: ZCMI, Salt Lake City, UT
      Mike Stevens, Visual Director
      Wendy Krobbe, Design

B

C

Suits — especially men's styled suits for women are shown here. Throughout the book we have shown suits for cruise — for fall — in navy — in black — in red, but here we stress the Menswear theme that seems to return with cyclical regularity.

The gray ladies in the Galeries Lafayette (A) are business women and they are ready to go out and take over the top corporate positions. To show their acumen and up-to-the-minute smarts about what is happening in the world, the window is stacked with piles of newspapers which though black and white does go gray from the distance.

Somewhat sexist — but still amusing — are the mannequins standing on the gray painted chairs in their gray and black, pin striped, suits. They appear to have been frightened by the stylized white mouse on the black patent leather floor. The gray setting is flushed with pink light that flatters the blonde mannequins and warms up their neutral colored suits.

There is no missing the message in this very dramatic presentation from ZCMI (C). The foreground is ominously dark and mysterious and beyond the angled and foreshortened doorways in the rear — there is light. Way off in the far left is a rotund, bulging dress form — like an overfed, Botero model who barely makes it through the slit-like opening while centered in the space is a standing and reclining figure personifying the menswear trend with shirts, ties and caps to go with the suits. The message is applied to the front glass and the pin points of light touch the faces and chests of the mannequins in this mood provoking setting.

Memphis 89 mi

Las Vegas 24 mi

Wichita 60 mi

Road trip 93

ZCMI's window (D) could be subtitled "Have Suit — Will Travel." And traveling is the game for the blonde mannequin and her piles of luggage. Her options are many as indicated on the sign post with arrows pointing out different destinations. The promotion "Road '93" is a stencilled on the front glass. A very smart and effective way to get a style or a promotion off and going on the road — as an option. Have you heard the one about the traveling salesperson?

D

A

A: St. John, Fifth Ave., New York, NY
Kelly Gray, Vice President Creative Design

B: Bergdorf Goodman, Fifth Ave., New York, NY
Richard Currier, Vice President of Visual Presentation

C: Lindissima, Puerto Rico
Frank Caballero, Display Designer

D: Marshall Field's, Chicago, IL
Jamie Becker, Director State St. Windows
Amy Meadows, Window Manager

B

I t's a take! The realistic figure in the St. John display (A) is suited and seated in a director's chair in this setting which recalls the old-time movie industry. All the cliches are here: the clapper, the reels of film, the kleig lights and the "antique" camera on a tripod. The background is frankly fake; it stimulates a street of facades with scaffolding for backing. The copy reads "Lights — Action — Camera" and the photogenic costume makes a star appearance in this cameo-size production.

Bergdorf (B) puts it to music and the Blues linger on in this nocturnal setting where the royal blue background carries a sketchy music staff and G-clef in gold. The floor is littered with music sheets and the mannequin in her tuxedo-style suit steps into the spotlight. A true performer.

D

C

With a bow to the black and white movies of the '30s and '40s, Lindissima entitled their mens wear-inspired fashions "Most Wanted" and played up the gangster films that starred such luminaries as James Cagney, Edward G. Robinson, and Humphrey Bogart. AND — just like they did in their "sheet-em-up" and "heist" films — in their double breasted pin-striped suits with cigars (that never lost the ash on the tip), these mannequins are surrounded by the loot in white canvas bags stencilled with dollar signs. Panels of "red brick" create the abstract setting and also add some color accents to the neutral colored merchandise.

Marshall Field's (D) does their bid for attention with rich, strong color. The red wall and the deep purple pull-back drape are washed with red, red light as are the figures in their menswear suits accessorized with shirts, ties and newsboy caps. More "men's"-inspired accessories and coordinates are displayed on the black and gilt etagere that also effectively raised up one mannequin off the color-stained natural wood floor. The composition is excellent and the two mannequins in the exact same pose work beautifully to balance the sweep of the drape on the left.

A

A: **Bergdorf Goodman, Fifth Ave., New York, NY**
    Richard Currier, Vice President of Visual Presentation

B: **Saks Fifth Ave., New York, NY**
    William Viets, Vice President of Visual Merchandising

C: **Galeries Lafayette, E. 57th St., New York, NY**

D: **Barneys, Seventh Ave., New York, NY**
    Simon Doonan, Senior Vice President Advertising/Display

B

Women's suits: feminine and flattering, tailored but soft, some with color and all are pretty. The traditional dress forms on ebony bases carry the same tailored suit in two colors in the Bergdorf (A) window. The mannequin is the prop — dressed in "lingerie" pleated and fashioned out of Xeroxed copies of a magazine ad and the same ads are twisted into cone-heads on the neckplates of the forms. One sheet is placed beneath the pink ribbon tied shoe of the mannequin. The white tulle pompadour adds another ballet touch to this simple, symmetrical, tailored presentation.

The three forms with the upholstered egg-heads in the Galeries Lafayette display (C) also are used to show off a single design in a selection of colors. The metal bases are more contemporary — as is the setting. The black and white checkerboard floor contrasts with the red back wall which, in turn, complements and clashes with the three featured colors. The cartoon balloons on the rear wall are filled with indecipherable hieroglyphics and doodles but they do get the shopper's interest. The fashion accessories are black bows on the abstract heads and the red/black and white shopping bags that are recalled in the window setting.

D

C

S aks Fifth Ave. (B) takes to home furnishings for the propping and the ornate period chair is turned upside down and held in its gravity-defying position by thick gold silk ropes finished with tassels. The pink and blue lighting not only tints the neutral rear wall, but it spills over on to the pink and blue textured jacket.

It is not a lamp sale at Barneys, (D) but a promotion for Prada suits in lit-up, sunny yellow. The assorted lamp bases look like refugees from second hand stores and Salvation Army depots in their '50s, '60s and '70s styling. The snaky electrical wires that slither along and clutter up the white floor add interest and texture to the composition. Note how the glow from the tilted lamp shades add to the light of the window.

A

The abstract in the wide brimmed natural straw hats are knee deep in the field of summer wheat as they show off their blue and white separates that combine bandana prints and solids in Bendel's window (B)

La Vie Provincial or Life in the Country, French style. The Galeries Lafayette (C) goes tres Gaellic in this sun-filled space in which the flat, painted basket of sunflowers is combined with the ochre/gold back wall and the natural gravel on the floor — all enhanced by the yellow light. The dress form wears a summer dress made of many prints and patterns of the Provence; all in blue and white. Fashionable accessories are set up on the rustic chair. Note how the yellow straw hat trimmed with ribbons and sunflowers floats over where the head should be.

B

Summer follows spring and often one just spills over into the other just as Cruise/Resort — which precedes spring — heralds what will be when summer comes. Summer is soft skies, sunny skies, sunflowers, straw and straw baskets, picnics and parties under colorful lanterns, days at the beach, walking the boardwalk, kicking the sand and tossing the pebbles, and dancing under the stars.

These summery set-ups featured light blues (also see Denim p. 60) and Laura Ashley (A) starred the headless figures in blue and white separates along with a blow up of the company's catalogue as a background panel. To set the summer scene, the "traditional" white wicker chair shares the space with a clay pot brimming over with foliage and miniature flowers. A few white louvered panels also suggest the Cape, a summer house, or the week-end getaway cottage.

A: **Laura Ashley, E. 57th St., New York, NY Barbara Kleber, Corporate Director of Visual Merchandising**

B: **Henri Bendel, Fifth Ave., New York, NY Barbara Putnam, Display Director**

C: **Galeries Lafayette, E. 57th St., New York, NY**

C

A

B

A &B show the Bergdorf way with colorful summer prints. Imagination and ingenuity take precedence over expensive props. For the fruit print (A), the realistic mannequin wears a straw hat and black shoes — to recall the black line work in the print design. On the white wall behind her are strawberries and a slice of watermelon cut out of seamless paper and artworked in black. The colorful prints and patterns in (B) are also accessorized in black in the all-white space. The mannequins lean on white brackets attached to the white wall and on the floor stand a collection of assorted size rectangles with the patterns, colors and prints that appear on the skin-fitting pants. Some of the prints are painted and some are appliqued onto the foam boards.

Harvey Nichols (C&D) takes its shoppers for a grand and glorious roller coaster ride in these abstracted settings that are filled with movement and color. It's a day by the sea or an evening out at the amusement park; it's a wild dare-devil ride which sweeps and swoops through the black window spaces that leaves bags and fashion accessories flying in its wake. It's carnival — it's a side-show circus. It's great fun and a great way to introduce the Swim wear that is coming up on the next page.

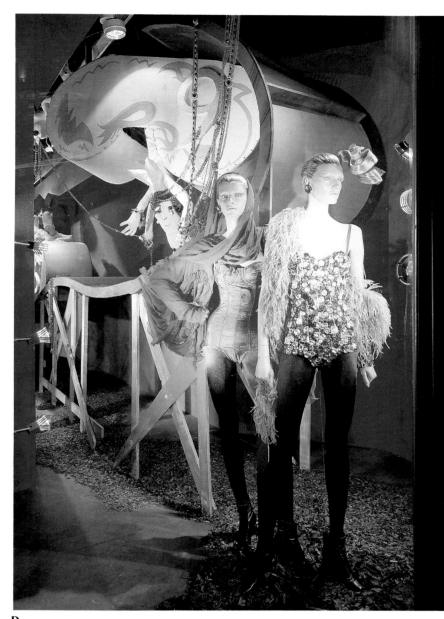

D

C

A&B: Bergdorf Goodman, Fifth Ave., New York, NY
Richard Currier, Vice President of Visual Presentation

C&D: Harvey Nichols, London, England
Mary Portas, Head of Sales Promotion & Merchandising

A

B

Come on in — the water is wonderful. So is the watery illusion created in the P.A. Bergner window (A). Who can resist the invitation offered to just jump in — to dive deep and to swim in and out and around the undulating wave panels that hang down in the blue illuminated ambience? A giant wire frame and silk covered fish rests near the bottom of the "sea" whose floor is covered with yards of crinkly blue/green acetate and dozens of iridescent glass bubbles. More bubbles polka dot the space and gold colored stylized mannequins in the latest swim wear fashions gracefully move about in this water tank window at Bergner's. The clear lights on the gilded mermaids make them gleam in this artfully constructed — and illuminated display.

Swim suits take on a naughty but nice attitude in this carnival setting at Barneys. The feathered head-dresses and boas may be more Las Vegas than Catalina — but the steamy and sultry setting — the draped wires of bare bulbs that lead into and through the mannequin group — and the very poses and attitudes of the mannequins all suggest a "carny" look that intrigues and attracts the shoppers on the street.

From Fendi — a pair of swimsuit set-ups. (C) has a great, big, fat snake of shiny black corrugated plastic tubing hanging down in the tall window and wrapping itself around the suits being shown; one on a stylized figure and the other on a ball headed form on a clothespin base. In true Fendi fashion the fashionable bags are color keyed to the merchandise and complete their own chain reaction as they slither down the mannequin's side.

The swim suits and cover-ups in (D) are all going "native": in style, in patterns, and colors. The "island" is represented by the smart looking black palm tree and the coconuts that have been shaken off that unlikely tree. The snake in this paradise setting is made up of brightly colored bags that are entwined around and work their way down the burlap wrapped tree trunk. Red and amber lights heat up Eden and make you want to strip down to the barest essentials.

D

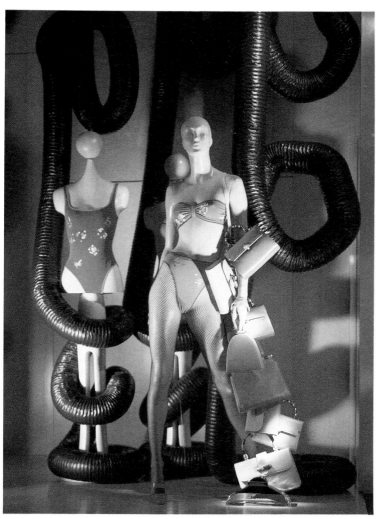

C

A: P.A. Bergner, Milwaukee, WI
   Charles Luckenbill, Vice President of Visual Merchandising

B: Barneys, Seventh Ave., New York, NY
   Simon Doonan, Senior Vice President Advertising/Display

C&D: **Fendi, Fifth Ave., New York, NY**

A

A: **Bloomingdales, Lexington Ave., New York, NY**

B&C: **Lord & Taylor, Fifth Ave., New York, NY**
Alan Petersen, Vice President of Store Design/Visual
Merchandising
William Conard, Director of New York Windows

You may want to refer back to Black (with white) p. 26 as well as Animal Prints p. 20 after studying these effective black and white swim suit displays — for a few more refreshing ideas.

The Bloomingdales' window (A) for the animal print suit plays up a multi-tiered background of cut-out foam board shapes that are supposed to be jungle grass but in the amber lit setting could be flickering flames. There is something "hot" and sensuous about this "cat" stalking the high grass and accessorized in clunky gold jewelry.

The prancing pinto pony (a repainted carousel horse) in Lord & Taylor's black and white swim suit promotion sets the pattern that is picked up on the printed suits in (B) while in the other window (C) the black and white spotted penguins take over to prop and play up the polka dotted suits: black on white and white on black. Consistent throughout the stretch of windows was the sunny ochre/ gold mottled and textured rear wall washed with amber light. Strings of bare bulbs were garlanded through the space also recalling the carnival theme mentioned on the previous pages. The platforms, pedestals and risers all combined sharp and defined areas of black and white with gold accents. Hats were the big fashion accessory here: black straws banded in white and baseball caps of assorted black and white prints and patterns. The shoes worn were white sandals, slippers and even dressy Chanel-style black and white pumps and Spectators.

B

C

A

The fantasies that dreams are made of — and that people dream their vacation spot will be. The L&T window (A) is a romantic place — far away — well off the traveled path — undiscovered except by a special few adventurers. Stone grottos, craggy tors, a palace built into the rocky firmament; sea shells are washed up from the azure sea that rises up at the horizon to blend with the equally azure skies. The two realistic mannequins inhabit this idyllic space in their turquoise swim suits and cover-ups while waiting for some tall and handsome Robinson Crusoes to wander by.

C

A: **Lord & Taylor, Fifth Ave., New York, NY**
   William Conard, Director of New York Windows

B: **Harvey Nichols, London, England**
   Mary Portas, Head of Sales Promotion and Visual
   Merchandising

C: **Bergdorf Goodman, Fifth Ave., New York, NY**
   Richard Currier, Vice President of Visual Presentation

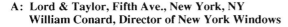

B

arvey Nichols bathing beauties are dressed — or undressed — for their trip to sun-drenched Barbados. Balancing them in the mauve colored setting is a twisted and tortured branch painted white — like a piece of blanched coral on which are entrapped some bright red sea-faring seashells. The ground, which is lost in shadows, is covered with sand and cotton roping is twisted around the "branch of coral" as a base.

Bergdorf (C) is saying that you too can have a wonderful time and wish you were there — if you had these swim suits which were designed to travel to far-off sunny places. Using the familiar Bergdorf signature of sandwiching the three dimensional figures between artwork on the front glass and on the back wall — the outline of the angled card is painted on the glass and the franked stamp and sun imprint is on the wall. The lighting provides the sunshine.

A

B

The world welcomes lovers — and loves lovers and everyone loves being loved and getting Valentine cards and gifts. So — is it any wonder that Valentine's Day — in late January and early February is such a delightful and delighting promotion? It comes before the spring and right after the clearance sales and brings with it color — and kisses. The displays on these two pages are all from Macy's Herald Square and they do offer a variety of approaches.

It may have started way back in Eden (A) when Adam realized that Eve wouldn't always be happy with just getting flowers — and covering leaves. The silky, heart-trimmed piece of lingerie is hung from a pink blossoming tree standing on a grassy spot in a rich, red ambience. There is no tempting snake in this idyllic setting but from the red patterned, white boxer shorts next to Eve — she knows that Adam has outgrown his fig leaf and going around bedecked in flowers just won't do. The flowers sprinkled on the ground — the lighting — the whole delicious concept reaches out to the shopper on the street who gets the humor that was intended.

Somewhat more "traditional" are the green ivy covered heart frames — lavishly coated with gold — that serve as backgrounds and the message bearers for the sexy red lingerie presented on three realistic mannequins. The gold oval mirror — far left — suggests a boudoir setting and on the floor is a build-up of cosmetics, perfumes, accessories, and other small gift suggestions. The sign on the glass: "A Time for Love."

How can you not fall in love with this marvelous Birth of Venus (C) — though with some apologies to Botticelli? The mannequin stands before the well known painting in full dimension with her coiled, curled and braided yellow raffia wig doing everything modesty can demand. This is not an X-rated display. The cherubs or putti fly around her carrying red, heart-shaped gift boxes tied with red ribbon. The sea shell on the floor opens to spew forward lots more Valentine heart boxes with red and gold ribbons. Imagine a whole stretch of windows based on "masterpieces" — each gently prodded and propped to tie in with the Valentine theme. Great fun.

C

A,B,C: **Macy's Herald Square, New York, NY**
Steven Kornachek, Vice President of Visual Merchandising

A

A&C: Lord & Taylor, Fifth Ave., New York, NY
       William Conard, Director of New York Windows

   B: Daffy's, Fifth Ave., New York, NY
       Mary Costantini, Display Director

   D: Bergdorf Goodman, Fifth Ave., New York, NY
       Richard Currier, Vice President of Visual Presentat

   E: Marshall Field's, Chicago, IL
       Jamie Becker, Director State St. Windows

B

Lord & Taylor shows off their black-at-home outfits in an amusing Valentine's setting (A). The giant, over-stuffed easy chair is upholstered in red heart fabric and the Kitsch/Kamp lamp shades and toss pillows add to the light-hearted setting. The floor is awash in pink confetti streamers and the red swag is pulled back to reveal the white French doors. Though it is set for Valentine's Day — it is a fashion display as is the one on the opposite page (C). Here the white target, pin-wheeled in black dots and accented with arrows set the holiday theme. The white dress trimmed with black and a colorful scarf is an early spring wardrobe addition.

Bergdorf also used arrows and target to show off their navy and white dream-team. The gilt and gray arrows are used to "construct" the L-V-E letters and the gold target that halos the mannequin's head serves as the O in the eternal message.

C

STEPHEN DIGERONIMO ON 3

D

E

affy's (B) doesn't ever take itself too seriously and they know their customers. The white stylized mannequins are dressed in black and red and accessorized with plastic hearts on red silk ropes — worn as jewelry. Each figure wears a crown of red and black playing cards shaped into towers and trimmed with red and black juicy gum drops. A large panel screen with a line drawing of a Botero-esque woman — in black on white with accents of red — backs up the threesome and the far back wall is appliqued with cut out red hearts marching up, down and across it.

On target gifts for Valentine's Day are shown in the Marshall Field's (E) display with a gilt cherub taking aim at the champagne bottles on the black and white checkered floor. Some arrows have missed that targets but the action goes on. White hearts are applied onto the rear black wall to make sure the message gets across.

A

A: **Lazoff, Puerto Rico**
   Frank Caballero, Display Designer

B: **Zaza, Los Angeles, CA**
   Design: RJM Studios, Los Angeles, CA

C: **La Grande Dame, Puerto Rico**
   Frank Caballero, Display Designer

D: **Fendi, Fifth Ave., New York, NY**

B

Lazoff (A) invites the Valentine Viewer to "Light My Fire" — and has provided the combustibles; hundreds of matches of dozens of striking match boxes to make it all happen. The heart on the rear wall is composed of appliqued match boxes and matches and more match boxes are glued onto white fabric and used around the bases of the forms and as a dynamic diagonal swath across the rear wall. The song title makes a great Valentine tie-in and there are thousands of other love songs out there that also say "I Love You" and "Be My Love."

Zaza (B) says "Be Mine" and offers the gigantic candy box created by the design team filled with colorful foil-wrapped "candy." The top of the box is also covered with foil — red — and trimmed with white and gold lace paper doilies. The box effectively screens the mannequin in the red and black gown in the open back window from the selling space behind.

D

C

To make sure that the message stated on the window at La Grande Dame (C) is getting across the larger-size mannequin, in a red and white holiday outfit, is suspended in the space along with a cut-out balloon trimmed with red hearts and string. To add another "lift" to the display, cut-out clouds fill the floor of the window.

It is RED for Valentine's Day at Fendi (D) and the handsome ball gown is shown on an abstract figure in the gold wood veneered window. On the rear wall are cut-out hearts with the names of famous lovers — and not so famous lovers and some red evening bags are caught in the spots of light on the wall. A black arrow points to the main build-up of assorted Valentine gift ideas beautifully coordinated and assembled on the floor of the window.

A

B

C

Go west young woman — go west. Going west often means going to the glorious Southwest: sand, painted rock formations, sand, desert blooms and cacti and more sand.

The sandy white outfits in the Bergdorf display (A) are shown against a "blue sky" and soaring in space is a recognizable cactus plant doing something unexpected in an unexpected way. The cut-out shape has been wrapped in crinkled kraft paper and tied up with sisal twine. The space is flooded with "sunlight."

For the gold chamois colored leather and the light blue coordinates, North Beach Leather (C) has covered its floor with white sand and simple stylized cactus silhouettes are stuck into the sand. Red cotton bandanas add a touch of color — as well as another "western" touch.

D

A: **Bergdorf Goodman, Fifth Ave., New York, NY**
   Richard Currier, Vice President of Visual Presentation

B: **Maesler, Munich, Germany**
   Peter Rank Design

C: **North Beach Leather, New York, NY**
   Frank Lehman, Display Director

D: **Sims, Ltd., Minneapolis, MN**
   Mike Vye, Display Director

From Munich, Maedler (B) envisions the West in terms of rough, hewn textures. The sun disk and the cacti are made up of rough wood slate nailed together and stained green. Nails, partially hammered into the cactus surface suggest the bristly prickers. Crumpled muslin provides another textural touch as it falls over the partial wall of the display window and sweeps over the floor. The mannequins in their "western" garb are topped off with cowboy hats and wear gun belts as a fashion accessory.

(D) simulates a bunk house or rustic cabin in the woods with this vignette setting made up of weathered planks of wood, a window frame and some bare tree branches. Jackets and carefully-coordinated patterned sweaters share the fall scene.

A

B

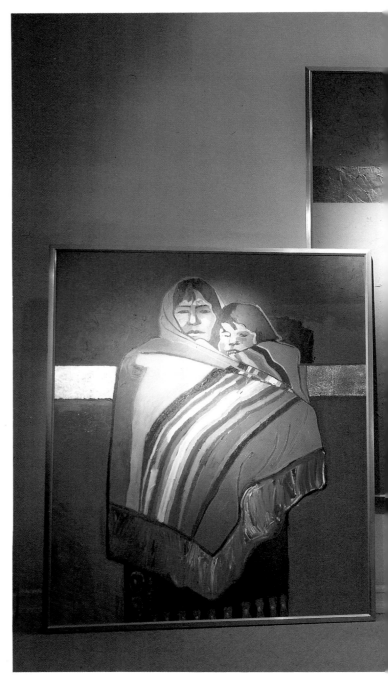

C

A&B: North Beach Leather, Madison Ave., New York, NY
Frank Lehman, Display Director

C: Lord & Taylor, Fifth Ave., New York, NY
Alan Petersen, Vice President Store Design/Visual
Merchandising
William Conard, Director of New York Windows

The West means cowboys and the Native Americans formerly referred to as Indians. It's time for tur quoise and silver jewelry (see Jewelry p. 109) and bows and arrows — peace pipes and war bonnets. The totem poles of the Northwest tribes inspired North Beach Leather's display (A) where the mask-like faces worked into the backs of the leather jackets and the flapping sleeves — all piled up one atop the other — set the totem pole theme. Bough of pine are spread out on the floor under the totem pole. And — just in case you didn't make the association, the feathered war bonnet on the reclining manne-quin in yellow gets the viewer back on the trail.

Right on the trail — and tracking just fine is this band of modern day "warriors" or "braves" with bows and arrows and "war painted" jackets. They have found the object of their hunt — almost hidden now by the hulking hunks — some with pony tails. She is the princess of another tribe — or you can write your own western soap opera.

The Lord & Taylor (C) Westward Ho! display was an artistic achievement. In their window they featured several wonderfully strong and vividly-colored paintings of Native Americans in rich color with royal blue predominating. The mannequins were dressed in white and pale blue denim — some with cowboy boots and others with cowboy hats. The fine lighting plan not only starred the light colored outfits but also enhanced each of the paintings.

A

Marc Jacobs for Perry Ellis on 2

B

ISAAC MIZRAHI
boulevard 4

C

The West can also be the inspiration for the setting of sophisticated outfits as shown on these pages. Billie the Kid never had it so good as these costumes designed by Marc Jacobs for Perry Ellis — based on a Western theme. Takings its scope and dramatic inspiration from the vast sunset landscapes in "Dances with Wolves" are (A&B) which feature the realistic mannequins in elegant black outfits shown against silhouetted backgrounds with recognizable forms; wolves, steer, a floating cloud, a barn, a weather vane and a water shed. A great part of the beauty of these displays was the superb sunset lighting in red, amber and blue filtered light on the rear wall — over and around the black masses defined by the polychromatic sky.

The black leather vest/bustier and white evening suit by Mizrahi in Bloomingdales' window (C) gets a Western hoe-down setting with the use of some raw wood horses and bales of hay bound up with black ribbon. The creamy white and black outfit is warmly tinged with the yellow light as is the straw — and the light colored wood. The unexpected juxtapositioning of the fine evening wear with the down-on-the-range props make this one work.

St. John (D) goes way out West with this setting of bales of hay piled high and the floor and back wall textured with woven straw mats. The realistic figure in black is lavishly accessorized with silver and jet jewelry and belts and she can probably do a mean rope trick — if given a chance.

A&B: Saks Fifth Ave., New York, NY
William Viets, Vice President of Visual Merchandising

C: Bloomingdales, Lexington Ave., New York, NY

D: St. John, Fifth Ave., New York, NY
Kelly Gray, Vice President, Creative Director

D

W e wend our way to the end with White which has appeared up in front with Black — with Bridal — with Cruise, and with many other promotions.

The birthday or bridal cakes — all-white icing tinged with pink were part of Bergdorf's bridal windows (See Bridal p. ??) and here is the honeymoon trousseau (A), smart and tailored in creamy white. The wonderful red wigs add just enough fire to warm up this gentle, almost white-on-white display.

A contrast in styles: realistic mannequins in Macy's display (B) wear white costumes while the stylized mannequins, painted gray, wear gray outfits — way back in the shadows of the window. The sharp light brings the two figures in white way up to the viewer while the "gray" people are allowed to recede in the space.

Black and white graphic panels on a lavender wall back up the semi-realistic mannequins in their simple white and off-white dresses. The strong graphics are held in check by the shadows they are in while, here too, the light defines the figures and their outfits.

The ultimate white contrasted with the ultimate black. Bendel's (C) shows their white evening wear on stylized, shiny black mannequins and the dresses are enriched with massive gold jewelry. An overscale black mullioned window frame serves as a background in this open back window and rising up from the glistening black diamond dusted floor are stark white branches. The lighting is on the white Oscar de la Renta gowns which step forward dramatically from the shadowy settings.

To make white a standout — it takes contrast and good lighting.

A

A: **Bergdorf Goodman, Fifth Ave., New York, NY**
   Richard Currier, Vice President of Visual Presentation

B: **Macy's, Herald Square, New York, NY**

C: **Henri Bendel, Fifth Ave., New York, NY**
   Barbara Putnam, Display Director

D: **Barneys, Seventh Ave., New York, NY**
   Simon Doonan, Senior Vice President, Advertising/Display

B

D

C

ABOUT THE EDITOR

Martin M. Pegler has long been considered a leading authority on store design and visual merchandising. He has been involved in the field for almost forty years and has worked in all phases of merchandise presentation: designer, manufacturer, display person, store planner and consultant. Witty, urbane, erudite and most persuasive, he has long been a vocal champion of store design and visual presentation as a necessary and respected part of retailing. This has made him a popular speaker across the country and for two tours of the British Isles, Mexico and Japan. He is in demand as a lecturer for industry, small business groups as well as, nation-wide chains and shopping centers.

Mr. Pegler is author of *Successful Food Merchandising & Display, Stores of the Year, Store Windows That Sell, Food Presentation & Display, Home Furnishings Merchandising & Store Design,* and *Market Supermarket & Hypermarket Design.*

He is currently a professor of Store Planning and Visual Merchandising at the Fashion Institute of Technology in New York and travels extensively, — always searching the field for new and fresh approaches, ideas and techniques to share.

MIRAGE

j. - walker

Madrid

London

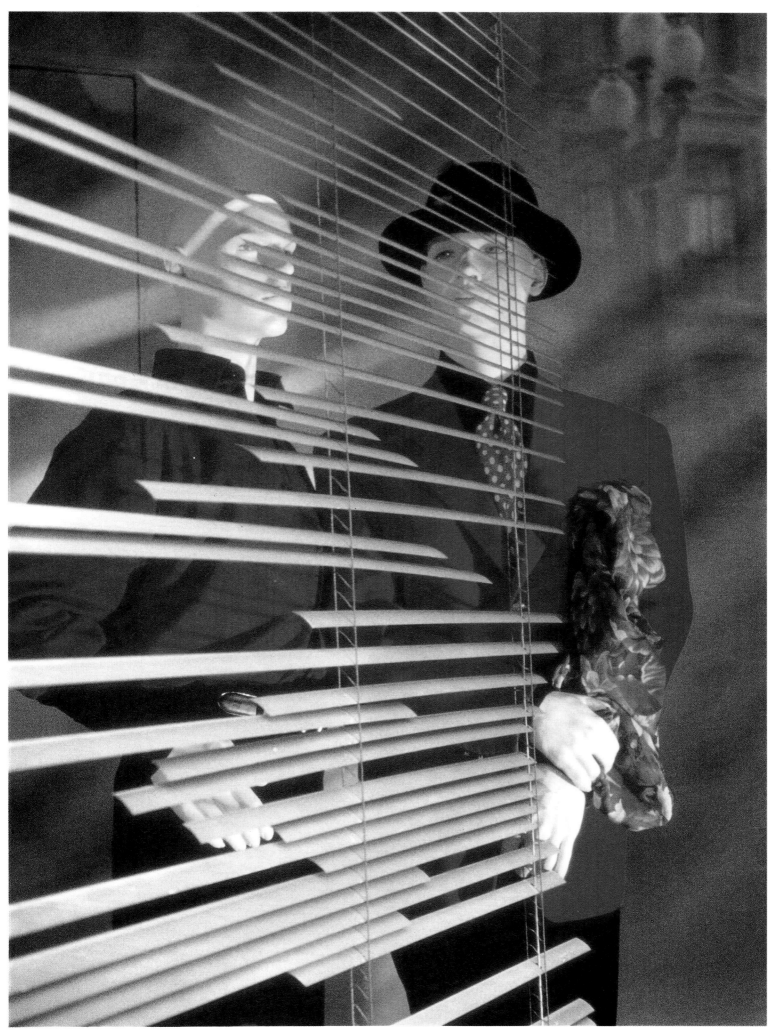

London

New York City

New York City

London

New York City

London

London

London

New York City

London

New York City

New York City

New York City

New York City

New York City

New York City

New York City

London